101 BEST BIBLE STORIES

101

BEST BIBLE STORIES

FROM THE OLD AND NEW TESTAMENTS

Re-told by

DAVID KYLES

and
Illustrated by
PAUL DESSAU

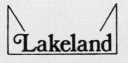

LAKELAND
116 BAKER STREET
LONDON W1M 2BB

First published 1954
First paperback Edition 1973

ISBN 0 551 00457 6

PRINTED AND BOUND IN GREAT BRITAIN BY
BUTLER AND TANNER LTD, FROME AND LONDON

AUTHOR'S NOTE

The Scripture quotations in the following pages are taken from the Authorized Version, but are frequently paraphrased where this was felt to be helpful. Particular passages are printed in italics. Capital letters are invariably used when reference is made to our Lord, except in quotations when the practice of the Authorized Version is followed.

The author is aware that consistency has frequently been sacrificed to simplicity.

Contents

THE OLD TESTAMENT

THE NEW TESTAMENT

Illustrations

Sorrow Comes into the World

The Bible begins by telling us that everything was made by God except one thing. That one thing has been the cause of all the sorrow in the world since.

After He had made the earth, the sky, and the sea, the plants, the animals, the birds, and the fishes, God made man. The name of the first man was Adam. The name of the first woman was Eve, which means "the Mother of all living".

God had already prepared a beautiful garden to be the home of Adam and Eve. Here He meant them to be happy and free from anything that could harm them. God said to Adam, "Of every tree of the garden you may freely eat: but of the tree of the knowledge of good and evil, you shall not eat; for in the day you eat of it, you shall surely die."

So the first man and woman in the world were perfectly happy until something came in to spoil it all. Amongst the animals was a serpent. One day, the serpent came to Eve, and slyly said, "So you have been told not to eat of the trees of the garden?" "Oh, no!" replied Eve. "We may eat of them all, except one. God has said, we may not eat of that tree, neither touch it, lest we die." The cunning serpent smiled and whispered, "You won't *really* die."

Eve listened to the serpent. The fruit looked very beautiful and ripe, so she plucked it. Then she gave some to Adam, and they ate it. Immediately, they both knew what sin and shame were. Everything became different, and they were no longer the happy people they had been before.

The happiest times in that pleasant home had been when they walked and talked with God in the Garden. Now they hid from God, for they were ashamed and afraid. When God called to them, "Where are you?", Adam replied, "I was afraid and I hid myself." "Have you eaten of the fruit of the forbidden tree?" God asked him. "The woman gave me the fruit and I ate it," confessed Adam. "What is this dreadful thing you have done?" God asked the woman. "The serpent deceived me," said Eve, "so I ate of the fruit." Thus they tried to escape blame for what they had done.

Then God said to Adam, "The earth is spoilt because of your sin; in sorrow and labour will you have to get your food from it. You will have to work very, very hard and by the sweat of your brow shall you live." So they were driven from the pleasant Garden-Home into a jungle world, and an Angel stood with a flaming sword to prevent their return.

Some time after they had left the Garden, Adam and Eve had two sons. The elder son was Cain, and the younger, Abel. Cain was a gardener, and Abel a shepherd. One day, Cain brought a present of fruit and offered it to God. Abel brought a little lamb.

God was pleased with Abel's offering but not with Cain's. Cain felt very angry, but God said to him, "Why are you angry? If you give willingly, I will accept your offering also."

Cain grew more and more jealous of his brother, and, picking a quarrel with him, killed him one day in the field. "Where is Abel, your brother?" God asked him. "I don't know," replied Cain. "Am I my brother's keeper?" "Your brother's blood cries out to Me from the ground," God replied. So Cain's wicked deed was known, and he had to wander about with the murderer's mark upon his brow.

So sin and sorrow came into the world together because of Adam's disobedience. But the story of the Bible is the story of how sin and sorrow may be done away.

The Great Flood

The sin caused by Adam's disobedience spread and spread throughout the world until God was sorry He had made man at all. But one good man—Noah—pleased God.

16

The dove brings an olive leaf back to the Ark.

One day, God said to him, "Noah, the world is so wicked that I must make it clean again. I want you to build a big boat, and, when it is ready, get into it yourself with your wife, your three sons and their wives. For I am going to send a great flood upon the earth that will destroy every living thing."

God told Noah how he was to build this boat, or Ark, giving him the exact measurements, telling him how to place the three decks, the cabins, the window, and the door. Then when the Ark was quite ready, Noah was to take into it not only his family, but also two of every animal and bird, and enough food to keep them all alive in the Ark for many months.

At last, all was ready. The rains came, and Noah and his wife, Shem, Ham, and Japheth, Noah's sons, with their wives went into the Ark. With them went two of every kind of animal and bird. Then, the Bible tells us, *God shut them in.*

The floods increased for forty days. The waters rose higher and higher until they were high above the highest mountain. The Ark floated on the surface, and all inside were safe, but everybody outside was drowned.

17

The rains stopped, but the floods kept swirling over the earth. Then they slowly went down. The tops of the highest mountains could be seen again, and at last the Ark grounded on Mount Ararat.

After forty days Noah opened the window of the Ark and released a raven which flew to and fro until the waters had drained away from the earth. Seven days later, he sent out a dove, but it came back because it could find no place to rest. Another week passed and then Noah sent out the dove again. This time it came back with an olive leaf in its beak. Still another week, and Noah sent the dove out a third time. It did not return, so he was now quite sure that all the land was dry. God then told Noah to leave the Ark with his family and all the animals and birds.

The very first thing Noah did on the new, clean earth was to build an altar and worship God. God was so pleased with this that He gave a promise to Noah that never again would He destroy the earth in this way, but that so long as the earth remained, seed-time and harvest, cold and heat, summer and winter, day and night would never cease. In token of this promise, God said He would set His bow in the clouds.

So every time we see a rainbow in the sky, we remember the promise given to Noah, and thank God for giving us our food so faithfully day by day, according to the season.

Abraham the Friend of God

In the ancient city of Ur, in the land we now call Iraq, there lived a man called Abram, or Abraham as he was later called. All around him the people worshipped idols, but Abram worshipped the only true God. So he left the city of the idols and travelled 500 miles north to the city of Haran which was on the great caravan road from East to West.

It was at Haran that God told Abram to leave his own

country and friends for a land which God would afterwards show him. Abram had no idea where that land was, but, obeying and trusting God, he set out with Sarai his wife, Lot his nephew, and a great company of servants, camels, and cattle.

For some time they travelled on, but, at last, God led Abram to the land of Canaan. There he was blessed by God, and became very rich in servants and cattle until it was difficult to find sufficient grass and water for all the flocks and herds.

Abram's herdsmen and Lot's herdsmen began to quarrel for the best wells and pastures, so Abram said to Lot, " Don't let us quarrel like this. The whole land is open before us. You choose where you would like to go. If you choose to go to the left, I will go to the right; if you go right, I will go left."

Now, Lot, instead of asking his uncle to make the first choice, looked across the lovely plains of Jordan towards the cities of Sodom and Gomorrah. He became so greedy to have this land for himself and his own family that he decided to stay there.

So Abram and Lot parted, but God encouraged Abram by telling him that one day the whole of Canaan would belong to his children's children, and that there would be so many of them that they would be like the sands on the seashore, or the stars in the sky, and that through them all the nations of the earth would be blest.

A long time after this, Abram was sitting one evening before his tent door when he saw three strange travellers coming towards him. He ran to show them the hospitality which is usual in Eastern countries; washing their dust-stained feet, and placing food before them. These mysterious visitors told him strange news. They had come from God to tell Abram that Sodom and Gomorrah were so wicked that God was going to destroy them both by fire. Then Abram remembered Lot.

He pleaded with God to spare the cities for the sake of the good people who might be there. If there were fifty good men there, would God not spare the two cities? God promised He would. Then Abram remembered that, because of the wickedness of those two Cities of the Plain, there might not be fifty good men in them. Would God not spare them for the sake of forty-five? Again God promised He would. For forty? pleaded Abram. For thirty? For twenty? For ten? Again and again, Abram pleaded, and each time God granted Abram's prayer.

Alas! there were not even ten, and Abram could see from his encampment the fire from heaven away in the distance falling upon the cities that had been so very wicked that their names are a byword to this day. But what had happened to Lot?

Two of the heavenly visitors had gone to the cities to seek out Lot. When they found him, they called to him, "Fly for your life! Do not look behind you, nor stop anywhere in the plain. Fly to the hills lest you are burned by the flames." So Lot, with his wife and two daughters, fled to the hills. But Lot's wife did stop and look behind her, and she was turned into a pillar of salt, because she disobeyed God. Thus Lot, because he had been so foolish and greedy, lost everything he had.

But Abram continued to prosper. His trust in God was so great that he was afterwards known as "the Friend of God".

*   *   *   *

Abram and his wife were growing old and yet they had no son. Then one day God told Abram that a son would be born to them, and that his name was to be Isaac. God also said that from this time Abram's name would be Abraham, and Sarai's name would be changed to Sarah.

Isaac means "laughter", and we can well believe that Abraham and Sarah laughed with happiness when Isaac was born, for he was a lovely baby, and grew up to be a splendid young man. Perhaps they loved Isaac too well, for one day Abraham heard the Voice of God in his heart saying to him, "Take Isaac whom you love so much and offer him up to Me as a sacrifice on the top of the high mountain which I shall show you."

In those far-off days, human sacrifice was not uncommon,

when men wanted to give God that which they loved best. But Abraham must have wondered if he had heard aright. How could God want this boy who had come like a miracle to them in their old age? How could the promise ever be fulfilled if Isaac must die like this?

Yet Abraham had always obeyed the Voice of God in his heart. So early one morning, Abraham saddled his ass, cut

On the way to the mountain of sacrifice.

wood for the sacrifice, and with Isaac and two young men-servants, set out for the mountain which God was to show him.

After travelling three days, they came to the place. Abraham told the two young men to stay by the ass while he and Isaac went up the hill to worship. Abraham gave the wood to Isaac, and, taking a brazier of live coals and a knife in his own hands, they started.

As they were toiling up the hill, Isaac said to Abraham, "Father, see we have the fire and the wood: but where is the lamb for the offering?" How sad the heart of Abraham must have been! but he answered simply, "My son, God will provide Himself a lamb for the offering."

At last, they came to the top. Abraham built the altar, arranged the wood in order, then, binding Isaac with cords, placed him upon the wood. Abraham raised the knife to complete the sacrifice—when the Voice called out of heaven, "Abraham, Abraham, do not lay your hand on the lad, neither do anything to him; for now I know that you really believe in Me, seeing that you were even willing to give Me your only son when I asked you to give him to Me." Just then Abraham saw a ram caught in a bush by its horns, and he offered up the ram in the place of Isaac.

How happy Abraham must have been, not only because his dear son had been spared to him, but also because God had been so pleased with this proof that Abraham really did love and trust Him. Abraham named the place Jehovah-Jireh which means "The Lord will provide".

A Bad Bargain

Twin boys were born to Isaac and his wife Rebekah. The elder was Esau; the younger, Jacob. Twins are often alike in many ways, but Esau and Jacob were as different as could be. Esau was red and loved to be out in the fields and the forests; Jacob was dark and preferred to stay at home. Esau was his father's favourite, because he hunted the venison his father loved so much. Jacob was Rebekah's favourite.

One day, Jacob was cooking what the Bible describes as "a mess of pottage", which was some kind of red lentil soup or stew. It must have smelt delicious, for just then Esau came in from his hunting, and called to Jacob, "Give me some of that red stuff, for I am starving." Jacob saw his chance, and quickly said, "Sell me your rights as the elder son first."

"Here am I at the point of death with hunger," replied

Esau. "What good is a birthright to me, if I die?" "Take an oath," said Jacob, "that if I give you my food, you will give me your birthright." So the strange bargain was struck. Foolish Esau swore away his birthright for a plate of soup.

Time passed, and Isaac became so old and feeble that he could hardly see. Feeling he had not much longer to live, he asked Esau to take his bow and arrows and hunt for some of the venison of which he was so fond, and told him that when he came back he would give him a special blessing.

Rebekah overheard this, and was afraid that if Isaac were to bless Esau in this way, the blessing might pass by Jacob after all. So she thought out a very cunning plan. She prepared a tasty meal for Isaac herself, and told Jacob to take it in to his father, pretending he was his brother Esau. "But," said Jacob, "Esau is a hairy person, and my skin is smooth. If my father were to feel me, I should seem to him to be a cheat, and he might put a curse on me instead of a blessing." Rebekah, however, had thought of all that. She dressed Jacob in Esau's clothes, and put the skins of little goats on his arms and neck, and sent him into his father's room with the tasty food she had made.

"Father!" said Jacob, as he came into Isaac's presence. "Who are you, my son?" asked the old blind man. "I am Esau," lied Jacob, "your first-born son. I have done as you told me; please sit up and eat some of this venison, and then give me your blessing."

"How did you find it so quickly?" Isaac asked him. "Because God brought it to me," lied Jacob again. "Come near to me," said his father, "that I may feel you, to see whether you are Esau or not." So he felt Jacob's arms and neck, and then said, "The voice is the voice of Jacob, but the hands are the hands of Esau."

Isaac also caught the smell of the fields from Esau's clothes, and so he was quite deceived by Rebekah's trick. He ate the food, and then gave Jacob the blessing which should have been Esau's.

No sooner had Jacob left his father, than Esau hurried in from the hunt, made savoury venison for his father, and took

23

Jacob receives the blessing which should have been Esau's.

it in to him. "But who are you?" said Isaac. "Why, I am
Esau, your first-born son," Esau replied. When the old man
heard that he was very upset. "Who was it, then," he cried,
"that came in here before you, so that I blessed him with the
blessing that cannot be taken from him?"

When Esau saw how Jacob had betrayed him, he cried out
with a bitter cry, "Bless me, too, my father." "Your
brother," said Isaac, "has deceitfully stolen your blessing."
"Is he not rightly named Jacob, the supplanter," cried Esau,
"for twice he has supplanted me. He cheated me out of my
birthright, and now he has cheated me out of my blessing.
Have you not kept a blessing for me, O my father?"

Isaac did give Esau a blessing, but, compared with that of
Jacob's, it was as the wastes of the desert to rich pasture-land.
Esau then determined that after his father's death he would
slay Jacob.

When Rebekah heard that, she warned Jacob to hide until
his brother's anger had passed. Making some excuse, she
persuaded Isaac to send Jacob away to her old home in far-
away Haran, to stay with her brother Laban.

So Jacob set out on his long flight north to Haran a lonely and unhappy man. Many strange things were to happen to him before he saw the old home again.

~~~~~~

Jacob's Ladder

Trudging along the dusty road, Jacob halted at many of the resting-places on the way when night came. At one of these he had a very strange experience. Arranging some stones on which to fix a kind of pillow, and tucking his cloak about him, he fell asleep, and had a wonderful dream.

He dreamed that he was lying at the foot of a magnificent staircase which reached right up and into heaven. On the steps of gold were angels of God ascending and descending. Jacob, in his dream, heard God speak to him from above the marvellous staircase. "I am the Lord God of Abraham," the Voice said, "and the God of Isaac. The land on which you are sleeping, I shall give to you and your children. Your children's children shall be as the dust of the earth. You shall spread to the west, and to the east, to the north, and to the south : and in you and your children shall all the peoples of the earth be blessed. I am with you, and will keep you wherever you go. I will bring you back to this land; for I will never leave you until I have done all I have promised you."

When Jacob awoke, he said, "Surely the Lord is in this place, and I did not know." He was full of wonder and awe at the brightness of his dream. "What an awesome place this is!" he exclaimed. "It is none other than the house of God, and the very gate of heaven."

He then took the stone he had used for a pillow, and made it a sacred symbol to mark the spot where he had seen this glorious vision. He named the place Bethel, which means "The House of God".

Jacob felt sure that in this strange dream God had indeed spoken to him to encourage him, and he continued his journey feeling happy and no longer afraid.

He made up his mind that throughout the rest of his life he would worship only the God of Heaven.

~~~~~~

The Two Sisters

At long last, footsore and weary, Jacob came upon a group of shepherds waiting to water their flocks at a well. Over the mouth of the well a large, heavy stone had been placed to keep the water far beneath clean and cool. Jacob asked the shepherds the name of the place, and, to his great joy, they told him it was Haran.

He then asked the shepherds if they knew Laban, the son of Nahor. They answered that they knew him well. " And," they went on, " here is Rachel, his daughter, with the sheep." Jacob ran forward to roll away the heavy stone from the well, and helped Rachel to water her sheep. He told her who he was, and she ran home to tell her father.

When Laban heard this news it must have recalled to his mind the time, years ago, when Eliezer, Abraham's chief steward, had come for his sister Rebekah, as a bride for Isaac.

Now here outside was this young man, Rebekah's son. Laban ran to find him and to bring him into the house.

Jacob was made very welcome in Laban's home and stayed there for a month or so as a guest. Then he offered to work for his uncle.

Laban had two daughters, Leah, the older girl, and Rachel. Leah seemed to have something the matter with her eyes, but Rachel was a very lovely girl, and Jacob fell deeply in love with her. Laban said to his nephew, " It isn't fair that you should work for me for nothing just because you are a relative. What wages do you want? " Jacob promptly

26

answered, " I will serve you seven years, if you will let Rachel be my wife."

Now, seven years is a long time, especially in the East where a man has to endure the heat of the sun and the cold of the night, and face many dangers, and Laban was a hard master to work for. But Jacob served seven years for Rachel: and they seemed to him but a few days, because of the love he had for her.

Then Jacob was given some of the bitter medicine he had given to his brother Esau. In the East, the bride is sometimes completely covered during the marriage ceremony so that the bridegroom cannot see her face. After the wedding service was over, and the woman Jacob had married lifted her veil, he found it was Leah he had married, not Rachel.

Jacob was very angry. He said to Laban, " Have I not served you these seven years for Rachel, as we agreed? Why have you cheated me in this cruel fashion? " His wily uncle had an answer ready. " It is against the custom of our country to let the younger daughter marry before the older. Serve me another seven years, and you can marry Rachel, too."

It is customary in some parts of the East for a man to have two wives, and Laban, knowing that, had planned to get another seven years' work out of Jacob. Jacob did work those other seven years—fourteen years in all—because he loved Rachel so much.

Jacob lived in Haran for some years longer, and had eleven sons altogether. Of these, only one was the son of Rachel. When this baby was born she named him Joseph, which means, " may he add ". This was really Rachel's way of asking for another son and, long after they had all left Haran, Joseph got a little brother who was called Benjamin. Jacob loved Joseph and Benjamin best of all his sons, because they were the children of Rachel. Later on, we shall see how this was to bring great sorrow to Jacob, and then great joy.

Jacob Returns to Canaan

By his skill as a shepherd, and shrewdness in all his dealings with his wily old uncle Laban, Jacob had become very rich in cattle and servants.

So much so, that Laban and his sons began to mutter and threaten. Jacob decided that the time had come for him to return home.

It was, therefore, a great cavalcade that moved out of Haran and took the now familiar road to Canaan. Jacob had every reason to be proud and happy, but for one thing—the vengeance of his own brother. Was Esau still angry with him? Jacob thought it best to find out before he ventured home.

He sent messengers out to where Esau was living, to tell him how God had prospered him in Haran, and to say that he hoped that Esau was no longer angry with him. They came back with the disturbing news that Esau was already on his way to meet Jacob, and had with him a band of four hundred men.

Jacob was very frightened, but he did not turn back: he thought out a plan. He divided his great company into two, and sent the first half on ahead of the rest, so that if Esau destroyed them in his anger, the remainder would have time to escape. Then he prayed, asking God to protect the women and children.

He selected a large present of cattle from his herds, and divided them up into several droves. To the herdsmen in charge of each drove he said, "When Esau meets you, and asks who you are, and where you are going, tell him that you belong to Jacob, who is coming on behind, and that these cattle are a present from Jacob to Esau." He then spaced out the droves with a long distance between each. His purpose, of course, was gradually to build up a good impression in the mind of his brother.

So he sent out all the droves and the first half of his company, and then the second, across the brook Jabbok, but he remained on this side of the brook alone himself all night. Then there took place one of the most remarkable scenes in the whole of the Bible. " *And Jacob was left alone; and there wrestled a man with him until the breaking of the day.*"

This mysterious wrestler found he could not overcome Jacob, so he touched Jacob's thigh and made him lame. But still Jacob held grimly on until the strange visitor cried, " Let me go, for the day is breaking." " I will not let you go," said Jacob, " except you bless me." " What is your name? " said the stranger. " Jacob," was the reply. " Your name shall no longer be Jacob," said the Voice, in the grey dawning, " but it shall be Israel, wrestler with God, for like a mighty Prince you have wrestled with God and with men, and you have obtained the victory."

Then Jacob said, " Tell me, I pray you, *your* name? " The Unknown would not declare who he was, but he blessed Jacob at that sacred spot, which Jacob called Peniel. " For," he said, " I have seen God face to face, and yet my life has been spared."

Who the mysterious visitor was, and what the strange wrestling could have been we do not know. Perhaps it means that Jacob was praying very earnestly that, as he returned to Canaan, he might be a different and better man. At any rate, from that time Jacob not only received a new name; he also received a new nature.

When the morning broke, after that dreadful night, Jacob crossed over the Jabbok, and there on the opposite bank was Esau waiting for him. But all anger had left Esau and he ran to meet Jacob, and embraced him lovingly. With tears in their eyes, they became reunited to one another.

One of the first things Jacob did when he returned to Canaan was to build an altar for the worship of God. He called the place by a name which means " The God of Israel ". In this way Jacob acknowledged that God had kept all the promises He had made at Bethel, when Jacob saw the heavenly ladder in his dream, and heard the Voice from heaven speak to him.

A Dangerous Errand

Joseph, Jacob's favourite son, was now seventeen and able, along with his brothers, to help in tending the sheep. Some of his brothers behaved very badly, and when he reported their misdeeds to their father, they hated Joseph bitterly.

They hated him even more when Jacob gave Joseph a special kind of coat which in Eastern countries is worn only by the favourite son and the one chosen to be the heir.

Joseph did not make matters any better by telling his brothers of two strange dreams he had. In the first dream, he and his brothers were binding sheaves in the field. Joseph's sheaf stood straight up, while those of his brothers came round and bowed down before it, as if doing homage to Joseph's sheaf. In the second dream, he saw the sun, and the moon, and eleven stars all bowing down before his star.

In Eastern lands, dreams are often looked upon as sure signs of what is going to happen some time in the future, and Joseph's brothers could not mistake what was meant by the dreams. "Do you imagine," they shouted to him in a great rage, "that you are to be our chief, and lord it over us?" Even Jacob chided Joseph. "What kind of dreams are these, my son?" he said. "Do you think that I, your mother, and all your brothers are actually to bow down and do homage to you?"

All the same, while his brothers were bitterly jealous of Joseph, Jacob wondered if God were not speaking to them all through the dreams.

Some time after this, the ten older brothers had to go out on a long journey to find grazing pasture for the sheep. They had planned to go as far as Shechem, about fifty miles away. After they had been away some time, Jacob said, "Joseph, I would like you to go to Shechem and see if all is well with your brothers and the flocks, and bring me back news." Now it was a long and dangerous journey, and Joseph had no reason to expect a warm welcome from his brothers, but he said bravely, "Yes, father, I will go."

The merchants bargain for Joseph.

When he got to Shechem, his brothers were not there. As he wandered up and down searching for them, a man asked him what he was looking for. "For my brothers," said Joseph. "Can you tell me where they are?" "Yes," replied the man. "They have moved on from here. I overheard them say they were making for Dothan."

So off to Dothan Joseph went. As he came near to the place his brothers saw him in the distance, and they said to one another, "Here comes the dreamer! Come on, let's kill him and cast him into some pit or other, and we can tell our father that some wild beast killed him. Then we will see what comes of his dreams," they sneered.

One of the brothers, Reuben, said, "No, I have a better plan. Let's shed no blood, but cast him into a pit, and leave him there." Reuben's idea was to rescue Joseph later on.

When Joseph came up to his brothers, they stripped off the coat which had annoyed them so much, and lowered him into an old, disused well that had gone dry. Then they sat down to enjoy the food Joseph had brought them.

As they were eating, a caravan of Ishmaelite merchants with their camels passed by, on their way to trade in Egypt. This gave Judah, the eldest brother, an idea. "What," said he to the others, "is the good of killing our brother? After all, he *is* our brother. Let us sell him to some of those merchants who pass this way to Egypt." The rest agreed to this —all except Reuben, who was away at this time, probably tending some of the sheep among the flocks farthest away.

Joseph was quickly hauled up, and sold to some merchants from the land of Midian for twenty pieces of silver. Soon after that, Reuben came back and went to the pit, and when he found it empty he was very grieved and did not know what to do. It was too late to do anything now. But his other brothers thought they knew what was to be done: they killed a poor little lamb, and dipped Joseph's coat in its blood. They then tore the coat here and there.

When they returned home, they showed the torn, blood-stained coat to Jacob. "We found this," they said. "See if it is Joseph's coat or not." "It *is* my son's coat!" cried the old man. "A wild beast has devoured him!" The poor father was so broken-hearted that even the wicked brothers were afraid.

~~~~~~

From Prison to Palace

Potiphar, the Captain of Pharaoh's Life Guards, was walking through the slave-market. His attention was drawn to a fine-looking young Jewish slave standing with head erect, looking all round about without any sign of fear. It was Joseph.

Noticing the Captain's interest, the Ishmaelite merchant put a high price on Joseph. But Potiphar paid the price, took Joseph to his home, and made him a servant in his household.

Potiphar soon saw that everything Joseph did seemed to prosper. One old translation of the Bible says Joseph was a "lucky fellow", but the real reason was that God was with Joseph. Potiphar came to see that it was better for him to leave the entire management of all his property to Joseph, which he did.

But Joseph was to learn something of the evil plottings that went on in oriental courts, and, because of lies and deceit, Potiphar became angry with Joseph and put him in prison.

Joseph was just as "lucky" in the prison as he had been in Potiphar's palace, for again God was with him. The Governor of the prison almost left the running of the prison to Joseph altogether.

There were at that time two important prisoners in the prison—Pharaoh's chief butler, and his chief baker. One morning, when Joseph went into their cell, he found them looking very glum. "Why are you looking so sad to-day?" he asked them, and they told him a very strange story.

During the night they both had dreamed peculiar dreams which filled them with fear regarding their future. "Tell me

33

your dreams," said Joseph, "and I will ask God to help me tell you the meaning of them."

The chief butler told his dream first, and Joseph was able to tell him that within three days he would be restored to Pharaoh's favour. The chief baker then told his dream, but, alas, for him it had a sad meaning. Joseph told him that within three days Pharaoh would order his execution.

The chief baker was sad, but the chief butler was jubilant. Joseph said to him, "When you go back to the palace, please do not forget me, but speak a good word for me to Pharaoh so that he sets me free, too. Tell him I was stolen from my own country, and did nothing to deserve being kept in prison like this."

The chief butler forgot all about Joseph, and did nothing to help him until two long years afterwards, when something happened which made him remember Joseph, who was still in prison.

One night Pharaoh, king of all Egypt, had two dreams which sorely troubled him. In the morning, he sent for all those in Egypt who pretended to be able to interpret dreams, but not one could tell what Pharaoh's dreams meant. It was then that the chief butler remembered Joseph.

He went to Pharaoh and said, "I do remember my faults this day. Two years ago, your majesty was angry with me, and put me in prison, along with the chief baker. One night we both dreamed strange dreams, and, in the morning, a young Hebrew servant of the Governor of the prison told each of us the meaning of our dreams. Everything happened as he said it would, for I was restored to my place, and the chief baker was hanged."

Then Pharaoh sent for Joseph, and what a stir took place in the prison that day! Joseph was washed and shaved and dressed in clean clothes, and taken into the presence of the mighty Pharaoh.

Pharaoh said to Joseph, "I have dreamed a dream which nobody can interpret for me. I have heard that you can tell the meaning of dreams." Joseph replied, "I can only tell what God gives me to say."

34

Then Pharaoh told Joseph, "I dreamed that I was standing on the banks of the Nile, when seven plump, fine-looking cows came up out of the river and grazed on the bank. After them seven other cows came up, thin and starved looking, such as I never saw in all the land of Egypt for poor quality. As I watched them, the seven thin cows ate up the seven fat cows, but remained as thin as they were before. Then I woke up. I dreamed again, and this time I saw seven ears of grain growing on one stalk, and they looked full and good. Then I saw seven other ears sprouting up, but these were poor and thin looking, blasted by the east wind. And the thin withered ears devoured the full and good ears. I told all this to the magic-workers of Egypt, but they could not tell me the meaning of the dreams."

Then Joseph said to Pharaoh, "The two dreams are really one. God has shown Pharaoh what He is about to do in Egypt. The seven fat cattle and the seven ripe ears represent seven years. The thin, starved cattle, and the dried-up grain are also seven years. Egypt is going to have seven years of good harvests and plenty of everything, followed by seven years of such terrible famine and scarcity that the years of plenty will be completely forgotten. The fact that the dream was doubled means that the matter will be sure and swift."

Then Joseph went on to advise the king what to do. "Let Pharaoh," he said, "appoint a wise and careful person and put him in control of all Egypt. Let him, under the authority of the King, have officials to help him to collect all the spare food during the seven years of plenty, and store it. The food can then be kept until the seven years of scarcity, and in this way the people will not perish when the famine comes."

The mighty Pharaoh felt that what this slave from the prison had told him was both true and wise. He agreed that some such plan as Joseph had suggested should be put in hand at once.

But where in all his great empire was he to find the man who could carry through such a colossal task?

Second to Pharaoh

As Joseph was telling him the meaning of his dreams and how to heed their warning, Pharaoh realized that God was with Joseph. "Can we find such a man as this, in whom the Spirit of God is?" he asked his counsellors.

Then, turning to Joseph, he said, "Since God has shown to you all those things that are about to happen in Egypt, there is none so good or so wise as you are. I shall put you in charge of my palace; all my people will do just as you tell them. Only on the throne will I come before you."

Pharaoh took the royal signet ring from his own finger and put it on Joseph's. This was the ring with which Pharaoh sealed all the official decrees. He dressed Joseph in royal robes, and put a golden chain of high office round his neck. He also gave Joseph the second royal chariot, and officials ran before it, calling to the people, "Bow the knee!" So Joseph became Prime Minister of Egypt, when he was only thirty years old.

Joseph immediately set to work. He personally surveyed the whole land, and set up a great system of store-houses all over Egypt. During the seven years of plentiful harvests, he stored up all the grain that could be saved.

Then came the seven years of terrible famine when nothing grew in Egypt and the neighbouring lands. Elsewhere there was starvation and misery, but in Egypt there was food for all. When the people cried to Pharaoh for bread, he said, "Go to Joseph, and do what he tells you." So Joseph sold the grain to the people, taking care that each person had only his or her proper share. It is the first system of rationing recorded in history.

Soon the cry arose in other parts of the world, "There is corn in Egypt", and long camel trains, and travellers on donkeys, and even many on foot trudging over the hot, dusty land, came seeking for food. And it was to Joseph they had to go—Joseph who had come to Egypt as slave and was now second only to Pharaoh himself.

Storing grain for the time of famine.

Corn in Egypt!

The news that there was corn in Egypt spread over the famine-stricken world. It even reached the camp of Jacob in Canaan.

"Why do you stand there looking at one another?" Jacob said to his sons. "Get you down to Egypt, and buy corn there that we may live and not die."

The ten brothers set out on the long journey south.

When they came to Egypt, like all the rest they had to go first to Joseph. When they came before him, they bowed down with their faces to the ground. Joseph's dream had come true. He recognized them, but they did not recognize him.

Joseph pretended to speak harshly to them. "Where have you come from?" he demanded. "From the country of Canaan to buy corn," they replied. "You are spies! You

37

have come to see the state of our country," said Joseph sharply to them.

"We are true men, not spies," they all protested. "We are twelve brothers; our youngest brother is in Canaan with our father; we had another brother, but he is dead."

Joseph wondered how really sorry they were about the brother they thought dead, and he meant to find out. "We shall see," he said, "whether you are spies or not. I shall believe you when I see this youngest brother you speak of. One of you shall go to fetch him, while the rest stay here in prison."

For three days they remained in prison, not knowing what to do, then Joseph, remembering that his father and all the others at home were hungry, said to them, "You may all return home except one; let him be bound in prison. The rest of you may go back with corn for your starving households. But bring your youngest brother to me, so that I may prove your honesty."

As they prepared for their return journey they muttered to one another, "This serves us right for what we did to our brother Joseph. When he pleaded with us to let him go, we refused to listen." Reuben said, "Didn't I tell you not to hurt the boy, and you paid no heed to me? Now comes the reckoning for his death."

They did not realize that Joseph was understanding all this, for he always spoke to them through an interpreter. Joseph went into a room and wept, as he thought of their cruelty, then he took Simeon and had him bound before their eyes. The others he sent on their way back, their animals laden with corn. Before that, however, he had told his servants to put each man's money back in his sack, and to give them provisions for the journey home.

At the first halt, one of the brothers opened his sack to get corn for his ass, and then shouted, "Look here! My money is back in my sack!" The others rushed to their sacks, and when they found their money had also been returned, they were very frightened. "What is this that God has done to us?" they said to one another.

When they reached home, they told Jacob all that had happened: how they had been taken for spies; how the great man had demanded to see Benjamin, keeping Simeon as a hostage; and how they had found their money back in their sacks.

Jacob cried out in great grief, "I am being bereaved of all

The silver cup is discovered in Benjamin's sack.

my children. Joseph is gone; Simeon is gone, and now you would take Benjamin. Everything is against me!"

Reuben pleaded with his father to let them take Benjamin back to Egypt with them. "Put him in my care," he said, "I will answer for his safe return." "Benjamin will *not* go with you," declared Jacob. "His brother is dead, and he alone is left. If anything were to happen to Benjamin, I would surely die of a broken heart."

39

Joseph and his Brothers

The corn was nearly all finished. "Go again to Egypt," said Jacob to his sons, "and buy us a little food."

"The man firmly warned us that he would not see us again unless Benjamin was with us," Judah, Jacob's eldest son, reminded his father.

Once more Judah pleaded with Jacob to allow Benjamin to go with them, promising faithfully to be responsible for the boy.

At last Jacob had to agree, so he told them to take a little present to the great man, and double the money, in case there had been some mistake last time.

So Benjamin went with the others to Egypt, and came face to face with the brother he hardly knew. Joseph ordered that they should all be brought into his house. The brothers were afraid this was because of the money found in the sacks, but Joseph's chief steward told them not to worry, but to accept it as a gift from God. He then brought Simeon.

When Joseph came home from his official duties, they presented their father's gift to him, bowing low to the ground. "Is your father well?" was Joseph's first question, "Is he still alive?" They assured him that Jacob was alive and well. "And is this your youngest brother?" said Joseph, and, turning to Benjamin, "God be gracious to you, my son."

Overcome at seeing Benjamin, Joseph had to retire to his own room, and there gave way to his tears. Returning to his brothers, he invited them to sit down to dinner. Joseph sat at a separate table, because Egyptians would not eat with Hebrews. Two things amazed the brothers: they had been placed at their table, according to their ages, and while special items of food were being sent to their table from Joseph's, Benjamin received better portions than any of the rest.

Joseph then told his steward to fill the brothers' sacks full to the top with corn, and again to put the money back in each man's sack. "And put my silver cup in the mouth of the sack of the youngest," he said to the steward.

In the morning, the eleven brothers set out for home, but they had not gone far when they were overtaken by Joseph's steward. "Why have you stolen my master's silver cup?" he demanded of them.

"Why!" they said, in amazement, "we would never do such a thing. If the cup is found in any man's sack, let that man die, and the rest of us will be the governor's slaves." The steward began with the eldest, and went down the line until he came to Benjamin's sack, and there, to their horror, was the silver cup.

Sad and puzzled, they returned to Joseph's house, and Judah spoke for them all. "What can we say? How can we prove our innocence? We can only submit ourselves to whatever punishment is ordered for us."

"Nay," said Joseph, "I will punish only the one who stole the cup. The rest of you may go home." Perhaps Joseph wished to find out if they would betray Benjamin as they had betrayed him.

But the brothers had learned their lesson. Judah said to Joseph, "We had to plead long with our father to let Benjamin come with us; if we go back without him, our father will die of very grief. I made myself responsible for the lad; let me stay in his place, for I could not bear to see my father's grief if the boy is not with us."

Then Joseph could not restrain himself any longer. "I am Joseph," he declared to them, "your brother whom you sold into Egypt. But do not be grieved with yourselves: for God did but send me before to save your lives by a great deliverance. Hurry back to my father. Tell him Joseph is alive and the ruler throughout Egypt. You shall all live near me in the sheep country of Goshen, and I will provide for you all during the remaining five years of the famine."

Pharaoh was greatly pleased when he heard the news, and ordered that a special wagon-train be organized to take food and presents to Jacob, and to bring him and all his household down to Egypt in honour and comfort.

When the brothers got home they ran to Jacob with the wonderful news. "Joseph is still alive, and is governor over all Egypt." At first Jacob could not believe them, but when he saw the wagons, he said, "It is enough! My son Joseph is still alive. I will go and see him before I die."

Then Jacob and his household, seventy in all, set out on the journey, and on the way God said to him, "Fear not to go down to Egypt, for I will make you a great nation there. I will go with you, and I will surely bring you back again."

Joseph went out in his royal chariot to meet his father, and what a wonderful meeting that was! Jacob said to Joseph, "I am content to die, now that I have seen you again for myself."

So the Hebrews settled in the land of Goshen, and were in Egypt for hundreds of years. All that time they grew in numbers and so prospered that they became a powerful community.

The Baby in a Basket

In course of time, the Egyptians forgot all about Joseph and what he had done to save their ancestors from starvation. All they could see now was that the Hebrews were becoming a great and powerful community.

The Egyptians became more and more afraid that in time of war the Hebrews might join up with their enemies and become what we would now call a fifth column.

So a new Pharaoh "who knew not Joseph" made oppressive laws with the express intention of suppressing the Hebrews altogether.

The more he oppressed them, however, the more they increased until, finally, he ordered that all Hebrew baby boys were to be drowned in the river Nile as soon as they were born.

Now, there was one little Hebrew family of four: father, mother, a little boy called Aaron, and his sister Miriam. Into this home was born a baby boy. He was so lovely that his mother hid him away to save him from the river.

When she could no longer hide him, she made a basket of bulrushes and daubed it with a tarry mixture to keep the water out. She put her baby into this basket, and floated it on the water. Little Miriam hid amongst the reeds nearby to see what would happen.

In a little while, Pharaoh's own daughter came down to

The baby Moses in his basket among the rushes.

bathe in the river. She spied the basket in the water, and sent one of her maids to bring it to her. When they lifted the lid, the baby cried. "Why!" said the princess, "this is a Hebrew baby," and she declared she would love to keep him for herself.

Clever Miriam saw her chance. She ran to the princess and said, "Shall I get a Hebrew woman to nurse the child for you?" When the princess said yes, Miriam fetched her own mother. "Take this child and nurse it for me, and I will pay you," the princess said to the baby's own mother.

43

When the baby was a little older, his mother brought him back to the princess, and she adopted him as her own. She called him Moses. "Because I drew him out of the water," she said.

So Moses grew up as a prince in Pharaoh's court, and as the Bible tells us later on, "*Moses was learned in all the wisdom of the Egyptians, and was mighty in words and deeds.*"

When he had become a man, Moses went out one day to see how his own people were living. He saw an Egyptian beat a Hebrew until the man died. Moses was so angry he killed the Egyptian with one blow, and buried him in the sand.

Next day he went out again, and saw one Hebrew strike another. Moses said to him, "Why do you strike one of your own countrymen?"

"Who made you a judge over us?" the man answered back. "Do you mean to kill me, as you killed the Egyptian yesterday?"

Moses knew then that his rash deed was not hidden as he had thought, so he made his escape before Pharaoh could catch him. He fled from the country where he had lived all his life into the land of Midian.

Sitting by a well, he saw seven girls coming to water their father's flock. Shepherds drove the girls away, but Moses took their part and watered their animals for them.

When they got home, Jethro, their father, said, "How is it you are so soon home to-day?" "An Egyptian saved us from the shepherds," they replied, "and watered the flock."

"Call the man in," exclaimed Jethro, "so that he may have food with us." Moses stayed with Jethro, and married one of the seven sisters. He was content to be a shepherd tending his father-in-law's flocks, and had no wish to return to Pharaoh's court.

But Moses never forgot the sufferings of his people away back in Egypt. Often when he was out tending the sheep, he brooded over their cruel hardships, and wondered how they could ever be saved from such terrible slavery.

The Burning Bush

One evening when Moses was away out on the lonely desert, he saw a very strange sight. A bush had suddenly burst into flames. This was no unusual thing in the dry, scrubby desert, but what was strange about this bush was that the more it burned, the brighter it blazed.

Moses said to himself, "I will turn aside and see this great sight, why the bush is not burnt."

As he approached the bush, a Voice spoke to him from the centre of it, "Come no nearer: put off your shoes, for the place you are standing on is holy ground." The Voice continued, "I am the God of Abraham, of Isaac, and of Jacob." Moses hid his face, for he was afraid to look upon God's presence in the flame of the burning bush.

God told Moses that He had seen the affliction of His people in Egypt, and knew their great sorrows at the hands of their oppressors, and that He had come down to deliver them, and to lead them to a land so rich that it was like a land "flowing with milk and honey".

But God required someone by whom to do all this, and that one was Moses. "I will send you to Pharaoh that you may bring forth My people, the children of Israel, out of Egypt," God said to him from the burning bush.

Moses, however, did not feel he was the right man. "Who am I," he said, "to go to Pharaoh, and to bring the children of Israel out of Egypt?" "I will be with you," said God.

But Moses was seeing all the difficulties. "When I go to the people, and tell them God has sent me to them, and they say to me, What is His name, what shall I say?" God replied, "I AM THAT I AM. You shall say to them I AM sent me to you."

"What if they don't believe me when I say God sent me?" Moses asked. God told him to throw his staff on the ground, and when Moses did so, it turned into a wriggling snake. Then God told him to seize it by the tail, and, when he did so, it turned back into his staff again. By this and other wonderful signs Moses could prove God had sent him.

Moses made another excuse. "I am not an eloquent man," he said, "I am slow of speech and of a slow tongue." God rebuked him for doubting so much. "Who has made man's mouth? Is it not I, the Lord? Now, therefore, go, and I will tell you what to say."

Even after all that, Moses tried to avoid what he knew would be a very difficult task, and God began to get impatient with him. "There is your brother Aaron," God said to him. "He is a good speaker. You can think out what has to be said, and he will say it, and I will help you both. I have told Aaron to meet you, and he is already on his way. He will be overjoyed when he sees you."

At that Moses submitted to God's will for him, and he returned home to tell Jethro that he must go back to his own people. Jethro was a man who knew much about God, and he understood. "Go in peace," he said to Moses.

So Moses, who had fled as a fugitive from Egypt, now returned to that land as the great deliverer and leader of his people.

~~~~~~~~~~~~~~~~~~~~~~~~~~~~~~~~~~

The Plagues of Egypt

Aaron met Moses on the highway to Egypt, and took the brother he had not seen for so long to his own home. There they prayed together and made their plans.

Then together they went to Pharaoh and said to him, "Thus saith the Lord God of Israel, Let My people go, that they may go three days' journey into the desert to worship the Lord their God."

Pharaoh haughtily replied, "Who is the Lord that I should obey Him to let the Israelites go? I know not the Lord, neither will I let them go." And he ordered his slave-drivers to make the Israelites work even harder than ever.

The Israelites had been employed in erecting some of the huge buildings for which Egypt was famous, and some of which stand to this day. When they made bricks, the straw to mix with the clay had been provided by the Egyptians, but now, by Pharaoh's order, they were to find the straw for themselves.

This meant weary searching far and wide, and yet Pharaoh said they were to make the same number of bricks as before. If they failed, they were to be beaten by the slave-drivers' whips.

When the Israelites complained to Pharaoh, he mocked them and said, "You are lazy and idle, and so you say, Let us go and worship the Lord. Get back to your work."

Then the leaders of the people blamed Moses and Aaron for all this new trouble and suffering. "Why did you go to Pharaoh?" they cried. "You have only made things worse for us."

Moses laid the matter before God. "O Lord," he prayed, "why has all this happened to the people. Why was I ever sent to Pharaoh when the result has only been more pain and suffering for us all?"

But God assured Moses, "Now you shall see what I will do to Pharaoh, for I will not only compel him to let My people go, but will also make him glad and thankful to hurry them out of his country."

"Tell My people," said God, "that I am remembering My promise to Abraham, and to Isaac and to Jacob. I will bring them out from under the burdens of the Egyptians. I will save them with a strong arm and with mighty wonders. I will bring them to the land I promised to Abraham, Isaac, and Jacob."

But the people were so deeply sunk in their despair because of Pharaoh's cruelty that they refused to listen to Moses.

Then God told Moses and Aaron to go once more to Pharaoh, and to warn him that if he refused to let the Children of Israel go, terrible judgments would fall upon Egypt.

Pharaoh was surrounded by his priests, astrologers, and magicians. When he saw Moses and Aaron, he demanded some sign from them that their God was greater than the gods of the Egyptians.

Aaron held in his hand a rod which God had told him to

Moses and Aaron before Pharaoh and his magicians.

take with him. He cast it on the ground, and it became a serpent. The magicians threw their rods down and they too were turned into serpents, but Aaron's serpent swallowed up all the other serpents.

48

Pharaoh still hardened his stubborn heart, and still refused to let God's people go, and then there began "the ten plagues of Egypt". God sent one terrible punishment after another on the unhappy Egyptians. While the plague lasted, Pharaoh would promise to let the Israelites go, but when the plague was lifted, he hardened his heart again. Finally, there came the last and most terrible of all the punishments which so broke Pharaoh's hard heart that he not only allowed the Children of Israel to go, but even begged them to go.

The First Passover Night

We have our Christmas and Easter: the great day for the Jews is the Passover. And this is how it all began.

God told Moses that on the night when the last and most terrible of the punishments was to fall on Pharaoh and his people, the Children of Israel were to take every man a lamb, one lamb for each household. If the house were too small for a whole lamb, then two neighbouring houses could share one between them, but there must be enough for all. The lamb was to be a very special one: it must have no blemish of any kind.

They were to keep this little lamb until the fourteenth day of the month; then, on the evening of that day, all the lambs were to be killed at the same time and the blood gathered in bowls. The head of each house was then to take a bunch of the hyssop plant, dip it into the bowl, and daub the blood of the lamb on the two door-posts and the lintel of the door.

Everybody was to stay indoors all night, and not go out. They were to eat the flesh of the lamb after it had been roasted, along with unleavened bread, a kind of scone or biscuit made quickly in a few minutes, because no yeast, or leaven, is used to make it rise like ordinary bread. They were all to eat standing, with their belts tightened, shoes on their

49

feet, and staffs in their hands, as if about to hurry away on a sudden journey—as, indeed, they were.

During that night, God sent His Angel through the land of Egypt, and the eldest son in every Egyptian home died, except in those homes which had the blood of the little lamb daubed on the door-posts. For God had said, " When I see the blood, I will pass over you."

Throughout the land of Egypt that night, from the humblest hut to Pharaoh's palace, there was loud lamentation. But the Children of Israel were safe and happy under the protection of the blood.

That very same night, Pharaoh sent for Moses and Aaron, " Rise up," he urged them, " and get you forth from my country from among my people. Take your flocks and your herds, and ask God to forgive me and bless me."

All the Egyptians were now eager to let the Israelites go. This, the last of God's judgments on Egypt, proved to them that the God of the Israelites was a living God. They loaded the Israelites with gifts of silver and gold and many things they required for their journey, only too anxious to get them started on their way. They did not stop to think how all the work would be done when their slaves had gone.

The Children of Israel snatched up their belongings in bundles, and, laden with their goods, and leading their flocks and herds, they marched out of Egypt, a great, mixed multitude of men and women, girls and boys. Moses and Aaron were in front, leading the way towards the land of freedom : the land " flowing with milk and honey ".

That wonderful night was called " The Passover ", because God had said, " When I see the blood I will *pass over* you." Once a year, every Hebrew family gathers round the " paschal lamb ", as it is called. They still eat it in remembrance of that night 3,000 years ago when God delivered their nation out of the land of bondage in so marvellous a manner. The Jews look back to that great event as the night their nation was born and they became a people distinct from all the other peoples of the earth.

Marching Through the Sea

The only road from Egypt to the Promised Land ran through that narrow strip of desert which separates the Mediterranean Sea from the Red Sea. The Children of Israel followed the shore of the Red Sea, and made their first halt at a place near where the Suez Canal now joins it. There they meant to rest and rearrange their ranks.

They had not long left Egypt when Pharaoh and some of his people changed their minds again, and were angry with themselves for letting the Israelites go at all.

Pharaoh hurriedly gathered a large army of swift war-chariots, and pursued after the Children of Israel to bring them back to serve as slaves once more.

When the Children of Israel saw this great army away in

The Israelites pass through the Red Sea.

the distance, they were filled with terror, and cried to Moses, "Why didn't you leave us alone to serve the Egyptians? It had been better for us to be slaves in Egypt than dead people in the wilderness."

Their position did seem serious. Pharaoh thought he had trapped them. On three sides was the desert, and, on the other side, the Red Sea.

But Moses said to them, "Fear not, wait and see the salvation of the Lord which He will show you this day : for the Egyptians which you see now, you will never see any more. The Lord will fight for you; you have only to keep quiet and at peace."

God said to Moses, "Tell the Children of Israel to go forward. Then stretch your rod out over the sea and divide the sea into two, so that the Children of Israel shall walk on dry ground through the sea."

Then God's Angel took up a position behind the Israelites so that, while he was a cloud of light to them, he was a cloud of darkness to the Egyptians.

Moses stretched his rod over the sea, and God sent a strong wind which rolled the sea back, and the Children of Israel marched right over on the bed of the sea. On either side of them was a high wall of water, but the ground beneath their feet was dry land.

Pharaoh and his chariots pursued after them into the sea, but their heavy chariot wheels sank into the sand so that they could not catch up with the Israelites.

When the Children of Israel were all safely over and on the other side, God told Moses to stretch his rod over the sea again, and the two walls of water crashed down on the Egyptians, and Pharaoh and all his soldiers were drowned.

From the far shore of the Red Sea, the Children of Israel saw in the morning light how God had yet again and for ever delivered them out of the hands of their cruel oppressors, and they burst into a triumphant psalm of praise and thanksgiving :

"*We will sing unto the Lord, for He hath triumphed gloriously: the horse and his rider has He thrown into the sea.*

The Lord is our strength and song, and He is become our salvation. Pharaoh's chariots and his host has He cast into the sea: his chosen captains also are drowned in the Red Sea. The depths have covered them: they sank into the bottom as a stone."

God's Great Provision

Even to-day when travellers venture to cross the desert there are three things they must provide for: a guide who knows the way over the trackless sands; water and food which are not easily to be found in the dry and barren wilderness, where springs and wells are very few.

The Children of Israel had none of these things. But God was with them.

First of all, God guided them through the trackless desert and by ways which avoided war-like enemies. This He did by a cloud shaped like a pillar. By day, it was a dark cloud against the sky; by night, it was a pillar of fire. When the pillar of cloud or fire stayed still, the Children of Israel remained in their camp; when it moved on, they folded their tents, and followed after it.

All this was done in good order. The people were instructed how to place themselves in position, and how to move out in turn as signals were given by the priests on silver trumpets. In this way God was teaching and training them.

The cloudy and fiery pillar was not only a sign to them that God was with them, but it was also a sign to the nations all around them.

Secondly, food was scarce in the desert, and the Children of Israel would have been very hungry many times if God had not sent them food. Once, when they complained that whereas they used to have plenty of bread in Egypt they

53

were now likely to die of hunger, God sent them "bread from heaven".

One morning, when the Children of Israel went out from their tents, they saw the whole ground was white. It was not snow, however, but a layer of tiny round wafers or seeds. They cried out "Manna!" which means "What is it?" and it was always called manna after that.

They could eat it as it was, or bake it into cakes, or cook it with other food, and it kept them well-fed all the long time they were in the desert.

Early in the morning, before the hot sun could melt it, some member of the family, perhaps a boy or a girl, or both together, went out to gather the manna for the household, six pint-cupfuls for each person.

It had to be collected every morning, for it did not remain fresh overnight. On the sixth day, a double portion was gathered, for no manna fell on the seventh day, which was the sabbath day. This double portion kept wholesome for two days.

After a time, the Children of Israel got tired of this food, and complained they never had flesh to eat. They were always grumbling to Moses until he got utterly weary of it all. "Why have I been afflicted like this?" he said to God. "What have I done that the burden of all this people should have been laid upon me. I am not able to bear it alone."

God took pity on His servant Moses and told him to select seventy of the elders of the people, and God would put a wise spirit on them, as He had on Moses, so that they could help Moses.

God was very displeased with the people, and said He would give them the flesh they had asked for until they loathed the sight of it. God sent a strong wind which brought flock after flock of little birds called quails until the ground was covered with them. After about one month, the Children of Israel had had more than enough.

The third thing that was difficult to get in the desert was, of course, water. Early in their journey from Egypt they came to a place which was called Marah, because the water there was bitter. When the Children of Israel grumbled about the bitterness of the water, God told Moses to take a certain kind of tree and cast it into the water, and the water became sweet and nice to drink.

Another time, when they had gone far into the desert where there were only sand and stones, again they grumbled against Moses because there was no water. They complained that in Egypt they had not only water but lovely juicy fruit as well.

God told Moses to assemble the people before a huge rock in the desert. With his rod in hand, Moses was to speak to the rock, and a stream of water would immediately gush out from it.

But Moses was so angry with the people for always grumbling and talking about how well off they were in Egypt, that he struck the rock with his rod instead of simply speaking to it.

The water gushed out just the same, and all the people, and also all their animals, could drink their fill. But the consequences were sad for Moses. God said to him, "Because you smote the rock and did not speak to it as I told you to do, you will lead the people to the Promised Land, but will not go into it yourself."

Mount Sinai

The Israelites had marched far into the desert and had come to one of the most famous mountains in the world, Mount Sinai.

Through His servant Moses God spoke to them from this mountain. "You have seen what I did to the Egyptians, and how I have borne you through the desert to this place, as an eagle carries her young. Now, if you will obey my voice, and keep my covenant, then you shall be a people

specially dear unto me above all other people. You shall be
unto me as a kingdom of priests, and an holy nation."

When Moses told the people all these words, they answered,
"All that the Lord has spoken we will do."

God then told Moses that the people were to make themselves and their clothes clean, for He would come down on
to the mountain. After a trumpet had been sounded, no one
was to come near the mountain, lest he should die.

The mountain then seemed to smoke and flame, and the
whole ground quaked. The people trembled at the sight, and
fell on their faces before the presence of God.

Moses and Aaron and the seventy elders went near the
mountain, "and they saw the God of Israel: and there was
under His feet as it were a paved work of a sapphire stone,
and as it were the body of heaven in its clearness."

Then Moses went on alone to the top of the mountain until
he was lost to view in the cloud of glory that hung about
the mountain, and there he stood in the presence of the glory
of God.

Moses was in that cloud for forty days and forty nights,
and during that wonderful time God gave to him the laws by
which the Children of Israel were to order their lives. Moses
wrote down those laws, but there were certain laws which
God wrote with His own finger on two tablets of stone. These
were the Ten Commandments, which we ourselves learn in
church or school.

The Church in the Desert

Up to this time, the Children of Israel marched more like
stragglers than soldiers. But now they were to become like a
disciplined army. Each of the twelve tribes was given its
own position, and each family its own place, in the ranks.

In course of time they grouped themselves around the very

Moses was away so long that the people became restive.
When he reappeared they were worshipping a Golden Calf,
and in his anger Moses threw down the tablets of testimony,
which were broken. The wrongdoers were punished and
Moses asked for God's forgiveness. Then he returned to the
mountain to receive the commandments again.

57

wonderful and beautiful erection called "The Tabernacle", or, "The Tent of Testimony".

When Moses was on the mountain-top, amongst the many other commandments God gave him was this: "Speak unto the Children of Israel that they bring Me an offering: of every man and woman (and, no doubt, of every boy and girl) who gives it willingly with his, or her, heart you will take My offering. . . . And let them make Me a sanctuary so that I may dwell among them. According to all that I show you, after the pattern of the Tabernacle, and the pattern of all the fittings and furniture."

How glad the people were to build a House for God! They gave all that was needed until Moses had to tell them to stop —gold, silver, bronze, fine cloths, and skins, precious stones; rare woods; sweet perfumes and oils, and many other things.

God told Moses how the Tabernacle was to be built, and who were to build it. Two clever craftsmen called Bezaleel and Aholiab were to teach others how to work in wood, metals, skins, and cloths.

The Tabernacle was quickly completed, for the people were willing-hearted. It was really in the form of a tent, for that is what "Tabernacle" means. But what a wonderful tent it was!

The Tabernacle itself was surrounded by an Outer Court made by a huge fence of white curtains. This was about 150 feet long and 75 feet wide. The curtains were slung by silver hooks from 60 pillars of wood, sunk into bronze sockets on the ground. It had a doorway formed by a curtain 30 feet wide, embroidered in blue, purple, and scarlet.

The Tabernacle itself was about 45 feet long, 15 feet wide, and 15 feet high. It was made of boards overlaid with gold, and sunk into silver sockets.

The roof of the Tabernacle was made of four coverings. The inside covering was made of the finest linen, embroidered in violet, purple, and scarlet. Over this was placed a curtain of goats' hair; then a curtain of rams' skins, dyed red; and over this again, a curtain of badger skins to keep the rain out.

The Tabernacle was divided into two places. The outer

one was called the Holy Place, and the inner one, the Holy of Holies. These were separated by a large beautiful curtain, suspended from four pillars, and embroidered to match the innermost roof curtain.

On entering through the curtain-doorway of the Outer Court, the first thing to be seen would be the Brazen Altar, on which the burnt offerings were made. Beyond this, the Brazen Laver which was made from the polished metal mirrors given by the women. In this the priests washed their hands and feet before entering into the Tabernacle.

In the Holy Place, hidden from the outside world by a curtain, were three articles of furniture; the Table of Shew-bread, the Altar of Incense, and the Golden Candlestick with its seven branches. The first two were made of wood overlaid with gold; the third of pure gold.

In the Holy of Holies there was only one thing, the Ark of the Covenant. It was made of wood overlaid with gold. Its lid was a heavy slab of gold, and this was called the Mercy Seat. At each end of the Mercy Seat was a golden cherubim, or angel-figure of gold, facing each other with their wings almost touching and covering the Mercy Seat. The presence of God rested on the Mercy Seat, though no eye could see Him. In the Ark of the Covenant were kept the two Tables of the Law, a Pot of Manna, and Aaron's Rod, which once budded.

A large number of priests carried out the many sacred duties in the Tabernacle. Every item of the Tabernacle had to be taken down and carried when the Children of Israel were on the move, and reassembled when they halted, and this was done by the priests.

The priests were chosen from the tribe of Levi and were called Levites, but only those of Aaron's family were permitted to enter into the Tabernacle itself. One of these was chosen to be the High Priest, and only he was allowed to enter the Holy of Holies, and that only once a year, on the great Day of Atonement.

Aaron, the brother of Moses, was the first to be consecrated High Priest of Israel. His high-priestly robes were very wonderfully made to show the great purpose and glory of his high and sacred position.

Two items of Aaron's dress were of particular interest. One was the golden plate he wore on his forehead, and which was fastened to his Mitre by a blue ribbon. On this was engraved HOLINESS UNTO THE LORD.

The other was a beautiful breastplate of large precious stones. There were four rows of three stones each, and on each stone was engraved the name of one of the twelve tribes of Israel.

When it was completed, the glory of the Lord filled the Tabernacle, and from that time on the cloud of the Lord rested on it by day, and a cloud of fire by night. By this, the people all knew the presence of God was in their midst.

It must have been a wonderful sight to see this thing of great beauty and splendour in the centre of the camp. It would constantly remind the Children of Israel of the holiness and righteousness of God.

~~~~~~

The Animal that Spoke

As they came near to the Promised Land, the Israelites approached the borders of the land of Moab which barred their way. Balak, the king of Moab, was greatly troubled to see so large an army of people on the borders of his country.

He knew he could not defeat them in battle, so he thought of another plan. In those days some men were thought to possess special powers by which they could destroy people simply by putting a spell over them.

Balak knew of such a man. His name was Balaam. He sent a message to Balaam, "Behold there is a people come out of Egypt: they cover the face of the earth, and they have encamped over against me. Come now, therefore, and curse this people for me, for they are too mighty for me."

Balaam told the messengers, who had brought him costly presents, that he would give his answer in the morning. During the night, God told him he was not to go with the men.

Balak sent another lot of messengers; this time they were even more important persons, and brought even more costly presents. This time, God said to Balaam, "If the men come to call thee, rise up and go with them; but you will speak only the words I give you to speak."

God meant to teach both Balaam and Balak a lesson in very strange ways so that they would learn it well.

As Balaam was riding along on his ass, the animal suddenly turned off the road into a field. Balaam thrashed it back on to the road again.

They then came to a path between two vineyards with a stone wall on either side. The ass pressed up against a wall, crushing Balaam's foot. Again he gave the ass a cruel thrashing.

A little farther on, the poor animal lay down on the road and refused to go any farther. Balaam was so angry that he would have killed the ass.

Then God gave the ass the power to speak to Balaam. "What have I done," it said to him, "that you should have thrashed me three times? Have I not been a good animal to you all my life? Can't you see what is wrong?"

Then Balaam looked up, and there standing in the way was an Angel with a sword in his hand. Balaam fell on his face to the ground before the Angel.

"Why did you strike your ass three times?" asked the Angel. "I stood in the way, and the ass saw me, and turned away three times. If she had not done so, I would have killed you for being so perverse."

Balaam told the Angel how sorry he now was for being so foolish, and said he would go back home. But the Angel said he must go on, and must be careful only to say what God would tell him to say.

When Balaam reached Moab, Balak took him to a high place from which he could see the camp of the Children of

Israel. When Balaam saw that great sight of tents with the Tabernacle in the centre, he said, "The king of Moab hath brought me from the mountains of the east, saying, Come curse for me Jacob, and defy Israel. How shall I curse whom God has not cursed? or defy whom the Lord hath not defied?

Balak shows Balaam the tents of the Israelites.

. . . Who can count Jacob's multitudes? Who can number his millions? Let me die the death of these righteous people, let my last end be like theirs."

Balak was very angry at this, and took Balaam to another high mountain where he could not see so much of the scene that had moved him so deeply. But again Balaam could cast no spell over the Children of Israel.

"Behold," he said, "I have received commandment to bless,

and God hath blessed, and I cannot reverse it. Surely there is no enchantment that can work against Jacob."

In a great rage, Balak took Balaam to yet a third high place, but when Balaam again saw that splendid scene he broke out into a poem of praise : " *How goodly are thy tents, O Jacob, and thy tabernacles, O Israel. Blessed is he that blesseth thee, and cursed is he that curseth thee.*"

Balak was infuriated. " I called you to curse my enemies," he said to Balaam, " and, behold, you have altogether blessed them these three times. I intended to promote you to great honour; but your obedience of God has prevented you from receiving a great reward."

Balaam replied, " Did I not tell your messengers? If Balak were to give me his palace full of silver and gold, I cannot go beyond the commandment of the Lord to do anything of my own will either good or bad; but whatever the Lord says, that I say."

Then Balaam gave a warning to Balak that any nation which tried to prevent the Children of Israel from reaching the Promised Land would themselves be destroyed.

The Scarlet Cord

When Moses died, the leadership passed to his chief lieutenant —Joshua. He was a brave and skilful soldier, and it was a good general that the Children of Israel required most of all, now that they stood on the borders of the Promised Land. For there was much hard fighting to do before it could be wholly theirs.

Joshua had two great obstacles to overcome before he could take the Children of Israel into the Promised Land. One was the river Jordan; and the other, the great walled city of Jericho which barred the way on the other side.

But God said to Joshua, " There shall not any man be able to stand before you all the days of your life : as I was with

Moses, so I will be with you: I will not fail you, nor forsake you. Only be thou strong and very courageous."

Joshua then made his preparations to advance across Jordan, but first he wanted to find out how strong Jericho really was. So he sent two young men to smuggle themselves into the city, and spy out the land.

The two spies got lodgings in the home of a woman called Rahab. The king of Jericho got to hear about it, and sent soldiers to arrest them. Rahab hid the men under the flax which, like the other women of Jericho, she kept on the flat roof of the house, and put the soldiers on to a false scent.

When the soldiers had gone, Rahab told the two spies that she had taken this risk for them because she had heard of all the wonderful things that God had done for the Children of Israel, and she was fully persuaded that the God of Israel was the only true God, and that the Children of Israel were His chosen people, and would possess the land of Canaan.

" Now, therefore," she said, " promise me by the Lord since I have shown you kindness, that you will show kindness unto my father's house, and give me a true token that you will save alive my father and mother, and my brothers and sisters."

The two spies promised that if she kept their mission secret, she and all her family would come to no harm when the Children of Israel attacked Jericho.

Rahab's house was built right on the walls of Jericho, and she let the men down from the window by a long rope made of strong scarlet linen thread. She told them to fly to the hills and hide there until the soldiers had given up looking for them.

As they were leaving, the spies told Rahab that when the attack on Jericho began she should get all her relatives into her house and not allow anyone to go out at all. Then she should put a piece of the scarlet cord in her window as a token or signal, and no harm would come to any of them.

When the two spies reached their own camp, they reported to Joshua all that they had seen and heard and he made up his mind to attack the city.

The spies escape from Rahab's house.

The Fall of Jericho

Joshua studied the report the spies had brought to him, and then gave the order to advance. But his plans to capture Jericho were like no military plans before or since. The plans were not made by any man, but were given to Joshua from God.

Joshua told the priests to take up the Ark which was kept in the Holy of Holies in the Tabernacle.

The Ark of the Covenant had a golden ring at each of its four corners. Golden staves were passed through these rings, even when the Ark was at rest in the Tabernacle. In this way it was ready to be carried whenever the cloud over the Tabernacle lifted as a signal for the Children of Israel to move on another stage of their journey.

The priests now lifted the Ark by these staves on to their shoulders, and marched a good distance in front of the Children of Israel so that all could see it.

When the feet of the priests touched the waters of the river Jordan, the river dried up just at that very point. The priests stayed there with the Ark of the Covenant on their shoulders, until all the people had passed over, just as their fathers had done at the Red Sea.

The Children of Israel were now camped on the other side of Jordan, and the siege of Jericho had begun. Here again the Ark of the Covenant was to play a very important part.

God instructed Joshua how the city was to be taken so that none of the Children of Israel should lose his life in battle.

Seven priests, each with a trumpet made of a ram's horn, were to take the lead. After them were to follow the priests carrying the Ark of the Covenant.

In front of the priests with the trumpets was to go an advanced guard of soldiers; after the priests with the Ark, another body of soldiers were to follow as rearguard.

This procession was to march round the city once each day for six days. The priests were to blow their trumpets as they went, but no one else was to make a sound.

On the seventh day, they were to march round the city in the same way seven times, and then not only were the priests to give a specially loud blast on the trumpets, but all the people were to give a great shout.

The Children of Israel carried out these strange instructions, and on the seventh day, after the seventh time round, the trumpets gave a tremendous blast, and the people a great shout, and the walls of Jericho crashed down outwards, flat to the ground.

The whole of the city was put to the sword and utterly destroyed, except for the silver and gold and vessels of brass and iron, which were kept for the treasury of the Tabernacle.

But Joshua had not forgotten Rahab. He told the two young men who had stayed in her house to bring her out in safety, and all her relatives with her.

Rahab, because of her great faith in God's purposes, became a great and honourable woman amongst God's people. She married an Israelite named Salmon, and they had a son named Boaz.

In the Book of Ruth, we read how Boaz married Ruth. And in the Gospel according to St. Matthew we read that a great-grandson of Boaz was David, the shepherd boy who became Israel's greatest king.

And in the same Gospel we also read that it was of the line of the royal house of David that Jesus was born.

When the Sun Stood Still

God had warned the Children of Israel that the people of Canaan were so very wicked that they were to drive them out of the land completely and spare none. If they did not, the Children of Israel would themselves become corrupted by them.

The inhabitants of one powerful city, called Gibeon, knew

this, and they also knew what had already happened to Jericho and other cities. So they thought of a cunning trick by which to save themselves.

They selected some of their leading men to go as ambassadors to seek a treaty with Joshua. Knowing that the Children of Israel had been forbidden by God to make a treaty with any of the Canaanites, they disguised the messengers to make it appear that they had come from a country far beyond the borders of Canaan.

They dressed them in stained and ragged robes and patched-up sandals. They picked out weary-looking asses for them to ride on, and put worn-out saddle-cloths and harness on the animals. The messengers were to take nearly empty wine bottles made of worn-out skins, and dry, mouldy bread, as if their food had been used up on the journey.

They acted their part well when they staggered into Joshua's presence. "We are from a far country," they said to him, "and desire to make a treaty with you. We have heard of all that God has done for you, and we want to be on your side."

When Joshua asked them where they had come from, they repeated their story about the great distance they had travelled, and pointed to their tired and worn-out appearance, and showed Joshua their bread. "This bread," they said, "we took for our provision hot from our houses on the day we started out to come here: but now you see how dry and mouldy it is."

Joshua was completely deceived, and he was badly advised by those whose duty it was to ask for God's guidance. He granted a treaty to the men of Gibeon, and took an oath to preserve their city and all its inhabitants alive.

When it was discovered that Gibeon lay only three days' march away, the Children of Israel were very angry, and blamed their leaders for being so easily deceived, and for not asking counsel of God.

But, because of their oath, they spared the lives of the Gibeonites, demanding only that they would for all time provide slaves from among themselves to be hewers of wood and drawers of water for the service of the Tabernacle.

This incident had a strange sequence which showed how God was over-ruling such things for His own wise purposes.

The King of Jerusalem and four other Canaanite kings heard how the men of Gibeon had broken their alliance with them and had made a treaty with the Children of Israel, and they sent a great army to destroy their city.

The men of Gibeon sent to Joshua for help, and, because of the treaty he made with them, Joshua sent a strong army against the five kings. By forced marching night and day, he took them so completely by surprise that their armies turned and fled.

Joshua realized that this was a decisive moment. If this battle was won, the whole of Canaan would be won. So he pursued hotly after the five kings.

God sent help to Joshua by causing a great storm of huge hailstones which destroyed more of the enemy than even Joshua's soldiers did. Night was coming on, and the enemy hoped to escape in the darkness. But Joshua prayed to God, and then called out before all the people, " Sun, stand thou still upon Gibeon; and, thou Moon, in the valley of Ajalon." So the light of this great day was marvellously prolonged, and a great victory made complete.

During the flight of their armies, the five kings had hidden themselves in a cave. Without stopping in the pursuit, Joshua ordered the cave to be sealed up with heavy stones, so that the cave became a prison-cell.

After the battle, he brought the five kings out, and made them kneel down before all the army of the Children of Israel. He then told each of his captains to place his foot on the necks of the kings in turn, as a sign that the victory was indeed complete.

" Fear not," he said to his captains, " nor be dismayed; be strong, and of good courage : for thus shall the Lord do to all your enemies against whom you fight."

This might well be called one of the decisive battles of the world. For it not only gave the Children of Israel possession of Palestine, but it also determined the whole course of history.

69

The Cities of Refuge

Moses had been so confident that God's promise to the Children of Israel would be completely fulfilled that before he died he had divided out the country amongst eleven of the tribes of Israel. Joshua was now told by God to confirm this division so that there would be no confusion or quarrelling amongst the tribes.

The twelfth tribe was the tribe of Levi, which was the priestly tribe, whose whole duty was to attend to the religious affairs of the nation. They were distributed amongst the other eleven tribes by having certain towns allocated to them. From these they would go up in their turn to do their service in the Tabernacle. For the rest of the year they would attend to their own homes and fields.

Amongst these cities of the Levites were six special cities called the Cities of Refuge.

In those days, the law in regard to injuries or violent death was "an eye for an eye, a tooth for a tooth, and a life for a life". Whatever injury one man did to another, the other was entitled to do exactly the same to him. If one man killed another, the relatives of the dead man could put his murderer to death.

Sometimes, of course, one man might kill another by accident. For example, suppose two men were felling trees and the head of the axe belonging to one man flew off and killed the other, that was a sheer accident.

In such a case, the man who had accidentally killed the other could run to the nearest City of Refuge before the relatives of the dead man could catch him.

Once there, he would be perfectly safe until a trial could be held. If he was proved innocent of intent to kill, he could stay in the City of Refuge until the High Priest for the time being died and his successor had been appointed. Then the man could return home to his native town or village, and live in safety.

If, however, it could be proved that the death was no

accident, the guilty person could be handed over to the avengers of the dead man.

It may all seem very crude to us, but the six Cities of Refuge were one of the many ways by which Moses taught the Children of Israel not to take the law into their own hands.

After he had completed all these wise arrangements, only one thing was left for Joshua to do. That was to get the Children of Israel to make a great and solemn act of decision and dedication.

A great rally of the people was held at one of the principal cities called Shechem. There Joshua reminded them of all that God had done for them and for their fathers before them : how he had called Abraham out of the heathen city of Ur to live in Canaan. He retold the story of Jacob, of Moses, of the great deliverance out of the bondage of Egypt, and of the many wonders in the wilderness.

And now God had given them the land He had promised to give to them—a land for which they had not laboured; cities to dwell in which they had not built; vineyards and oliveyards to eat which they had not planted.

Now, as they faced the new future, Joshua called upon them to break with all that had been harmful in the past. " Now, therefore," he cried, " fear the Lord, and serve Him in sincerity and truth, and put away the idols which your fathers served in Egypt."

" Choose this day," he challenged them, " whom you will serve." And then went on to declare that he had made *his* decision. " As for me and my house, we will serve the Lord," he said.

The people all declared that they would forsake all idol-worship and serve only the true and living God.

Joshua raised a monument in Shechem as a memorial of this great decision, and wrote all the words down in a book, and then the people departed to the various places they had inherited throughout Canaan.

Joshua, all his great work ended, died at the age of one hundred and ten years, and he was buried in Mount Ephraim, which had been part of his own inheritance.

David looking after his father's sheep.

The Shepherd King

For a long time after the death of Joshua, the Children of Israel had no great national leader like Moses or Joshua to lead them against the enemies who hemmed them in on every side.

Each of those enemies had a King to lead them. So the Israelites clamoured for a King of their own. The first man to be anointed King over all Israel was Saul, of the little tribe of Benjamin.

For a time Saul did well. He was gradually overcoming all Israel's foes, especially the Philistines, a warlike people who did the Israelites much harm. But Saul took his own way far too often, until at long last God was sorry Saul had ever been made King of Israel at all.

The real leader of the people at this time was the prophet Samuel. Every boy and girl must know how Samuel was presented to the Temple of the Lord at Shiloh by his mother, when he was a very little boy. Now, he was a very old man and had served his people nobly.

It was Samuel who had anointed Saul as King over Israel, and now he was grieved to see how sadly Saul had failed to fulfil all the great hopes that had been placed on him, and how self-willed he had become.

One day God said to Samuel, "Do not grieve any longer over Saul, for I have rejected him from reigning over Israel. Fill your horn again with oil, and go to the house of Jesse who lives in Bethlehem, for I have chosen one of his sons to be King over Israel."

Samuel's visit to the little town of Bethlehem caused a great sensation. The elders of the town met him, and said nervously, "Do you come peaceably?"

"Peaceably," Samuel replied. "I am come to sacrifice to the Lord. Purify yourselves, and come and join me in the sacrifice."

When they were all present, Samuel looked at Jesse's sons, and Eliab, the eldest son, impressed him greatly. "Surely this is the Lord's anointed," he thought.

But God said to Samuel, "Do not look on his appearance or his height, for I am refusing this one : for the Lord does not look at things as man does. Man looks on the outward appearance, but the Lord looks on the heart."

Then Jesse called for his second son, Abinadab; and then the third, Shammah, but the Lord had not chosen either of these.

Four other sons were presented to the prophet, according to their age, but Samuel received no sign that any of them was the one the Lord had chosen.

The old prophet was very puzzled. "Are these all your children?" he asked Jesse.

"Well, no," Jesse replied, "there is still the youngest one, David, but he is out looking after the sheep." Nobody seems to have thought it worth while inviting this mere boy to the feast.

"Send and fetch him," cried Samuel, "for we will not sit down until he comes."

When David came hurrying in, he was rosy with running. He had curly auburn hair, and beautiful blue eyes, and a very striking appearance.

As he stood before the old prophet, wondering what it was all about, God said to Samuel, "Arise, anoint him, for this is he."

Then Samuel took the horn of oil, and anointed David before his brothers and all the others. As Samuel's hands rested on David's head, David felt that the Spirit of God had come into his heart.

All the others do not seem to have understood what Samuel was doing, and, after the ceremony was over, David went back to his sheep. But as he continued to watch over his father's flock, David never forgot that great moment. As he awaited the call of God which he knew would surely come, he quietly prepared himself for the great task that lay before him.

David and Goliath

The fiercest of the enemies of the Israelites were the war-like Philistines. War had again broken out between them, and the two armies faced each other across the valley of Elah.

One morning, the Israelites saw two men coming towards them from the other side. The first man carried an enormous shield. But it was the second man who made them all gasp. He was almost twice as tall as the man in front; he was much taller even than their own leader, King Saul, who was head and shoulders above all the other men in Israel. Not only was this man huge, he wore the heaviest armour and carried the largest spear and sword ever made. His name was Goliath.

Goliath roared out with a terrible voice. "Why have a battle at all in which many men will only be killed? I am a

74

Philistine and you are Israelites. Let one of you come down and fight me here. If he kills me, we shall be your prisoners; if I kill him, you shall be ours." And, then, in a louder voice still, "I defy the forces of Israel."

This performance was repeated twice every day, but all

David sees the Philistine armies.

the Israelites were very afraid, and no man was willing to face Goliath.

David's three eldest brothers were serving with the Israelite army under King Saul. One day, Jesse said to David, "I want you to go down to the army and take some nice things to your three brothers; also take some milk-cheeses to their commanding officer. Find out how things are going with them, and hurry back with the news." Jesse never imagined what kind of news David was to bring back.

When he reached the front, David found that the Israelites were getting ready to go into action. He quickly handed over his parcels to the storekeeper, and ran amongst the soldiers, looking for his three brothers.

Just at that moment, the great shout from Goliath came rolling across the valley. David listened to the giant's challenge, and then waited for it to be taken up.

To his amazement and disgust, the men of Israel fell back in fear, and David was ashamed of his countrymen.

"What shall be done," he cried, "for the one who kills this Philistine, and wipes out this disgrace from Israel?"

He was thinking only of the glory of defending the honour of Israel's God. But the soldiers told him that Saul had promised not only great riches to the one who killed Goliath, but also his own daughter for his wife, and princely rank to all that man's family.

Eliab, David's eldest brother, heard David talking like this with the soldiers and was very angry with him. He thought David was just being impertinent.

"What have you come here for?" he shouted at David. "Why have you deserted the poor sheep at home? You have only come to see the battle. Be off home with you!"

But some of the soldiers had been struck by David's manner, and they took him into the very presence of Saul himself.

Do you think David was too nervous to speak to the King? He was not! He could only think of the shame that had come over his nation. "Let not the King be afraid," he cried out, "I shall go and fight Goliath."

The King looked kindly on the eager young boy, and said, "You cannot fight this big fellow. You are but a youth, and he has been a soldier all his life."

David, looking up at Saul, replied, "I have kept my father's sheep. When a lion or a bear came to take the sheep, I took hold of it by the jaw and killed it. After that, I am not afraid of this Philistine."

Now, David was not just boasting. While watching the sheep, he had learned three things. First, he had learned how to play the shepherd's harp. He would make up little tunes

76

and put words to them, and some of the songs he wrote you will find in the Book of Psalms.

The twenty-third psalm, the Shepherd's Psalm, is one of them. Those psalms, or songs, tell of God's love and care for those who love and trust Him.

Secondly, he had learned how to use the shepherd's sling. He had acquired great skill so that he could hit even a small target at a great distance.

Thirdly, he had learned courage. An Eastern shepherd's life is a dangerous one. He has to protect his sheep against bandits, wild beasts and wild birds.

David had learned by hard experience to know that if he trusted in God, he need not fear anything at all. That is why he wrote in one of his psalms, *"In God have I put my trust; I will not be afraid what man can do unto me."*

When the King saw the earnestness of the lad, and, perhaps, rebuked by the boy's simple trust in God, he said to David, "Go, and may God be with you."

Then out of kindness he ordered that his own armour should be put on David, but it was too big and heavy for the boy.

"I cannot even move with these," he said to Saul. "I am not used to wearing armour," and he took it all off.

David then took his shepherd's club, picked five stones from a nearby brook, put these in his shepherd's pouch, and went across the valley to meet Goliath. The giant could hardly believe his eyes. Was this all the army of Israel could send against him—a boy with a club in his hand?

Then he got very angry, and roared at David, "What do you think I am—a dog you can chase away with a stick? Come on, and I will make you into food for the fowls of the air, and the beasts of the fields."

David's reply was calm and confident, "You come with sword and spear and shield, but I come in the name of the Lord of hosts, the God of the armies of Israel, Whom you have defied," he said.

Then he told the giant what he was going to do, and why. "I will smite you and cut off your head, so that all these

77

people who are looking on watching us may know that God does not depend on swords and spears. This battle is not in our hands but God's."

At that Goliath rushed at David in a mad rage, but David took the sling out of his pouch with one of the five stones, whirled the sling with careful aim, and hit the huge fellow right in the forehead.

Goliath fell to the ground, and David, drawing the giant's own sword out of its huge sheath, cut off the giant's head and held it up for all to see. When they saw it, the Philistines turned and fled. The Israelites chased after them, and won a great victory.

A Great Friendship

After the great victory over the Philistines, which followed upon the death of their champion Goliath, David was brought into the presence of Saul the King.

Standing beside the King was Jonathan, his eldest son. When he saw David, he felt that his soul was bound together with David's, and he loved him very dearly.

Saul would not allow David to return home, but kept him at his court, and made him a commander in the army. David soon became popular both with the soldiers and the people.

As the army returned home in triumph after a victory, the people would dance with joy, and shout aloud, " Saul has slain his thousands and David his ten thousands." Saul began to be very jealous of David because of this.

For a time, Jonathan helped to keep things from becoming too unpleasant between his father and his great friend David. But fits of jealousy would suddenly overtake Saul, and he would be like one possessed with some evil spirit.

Once after a great victory over the Philistines, as Saul and David were talking together in a friendly way, Saul suddenly seized a javelin and hurled it at David to pin him to the wall.

David made his escape from Saul, and sought out Jonathan. "What have I done," asked David, "that your father should seek to kill me?"

David and Jonathan, the faithful friends.

Jonathan could not believe that his father really wanted to kill David. "My father does nothing," he said, "without first telling me."

But David reminded him that the King knew of their love

for one another and, therefore, was not likely to tell Jonathan of his plans to kill David.

So the two friends decided to make sure about this. The next day was the feast of the new moon, and David was to have a special place there. They arranged that David should absent himself, and if Saul asked where he was, Jonathan was to say he had gone home to Bethlehem to join in a family sacrifice.

If the King seemed to be pleased to hear this, then David and Jonathan would know all was well. If he should be angry, then Jonathan would know for certain his father meant to kill David.

Saul did miss David at the feast, and enquired why he was not in his place. When he was told that David had gone to take part in a sacrifice at home, he fell into a terrible passion. He raged and cursed at Jonathan, and asked him if he did not realize that his friendship with David was treachery to himself and his family, for so long as David lived Jonathan would never be King.

He then commanded Jonathan to bring David to him, so that sentence of death might be passed on him. When Jonathan refused to do any such thing, his father was so beside himself with rage that he seized a spear to throw at him.

Then Jonathan knew that his father was determined to kill David, and he felt angry and ashamed because of his father's wickedness.

His only thought was to help his friend. But how could he warn David without betraying him, for he knew he would now be closely watched by his father's spies?

The two friends had thought of that too, and had arranged a very clever signal.

David was to lie concealed in a secret meeting place, and to watch for Jonathan. At the time agreed, Jonathan went out to the appointed place. He took with him a small boy to carry his bow and arrows.

When they got to the place where David lay hidden, Jonathan told the boy to run on ahead and pick up the arrows as he shot them.

As the boy ran, Jonathan shot an arrow beyond him, and then called out, " Is not the arrow beyond you? "

Then, as the boy was looking for the arrow, he shouted again, " Make speed, haste, stay not."

All this was the signal to David to go into hiding somewhere at once, for Saul was determined to kill him.

Jonathan sent the boy back to town with the bow and arrows, and David came out, bowing before Jonathan three times, thus recognizing that his friend was the royal prince.

The two friends took a loving farewell of one another. " Go in peace," said Jonathan, " for we have both taken a pledge that the Lord will be a bond between us both, and between our children for ever."

This friendship between David and Jonathan is one of the loveliest stories of comradeship in all the world. Their love for one another has become proverbial. When two men are loyal to one another like that, they are said to be " David to the other's Jonathan ".

*   *   *   *

Some years later, when both Saul and Jonathan had been killed in a battle with the Philistines, and David had become King, he remembered the pledge he had made with his dear friend. Jonathan died a hero's death, leaving at home a little son only five years old, called Mephibosheth. When the news of his father's death had come, his nurse had snatched him up, and fled to a place of safety.

In her haste, she had let the boy fall, and he was so badly hurt that he grew up deformed in both feet and could not walk very well. His hiding place had been kept very secret for a long time.

David now thought of his old friend Jonathan, and remembered how they had promised one another to look after each other's children. " Is there no one of the house of Saul left, that I may be kind to him, for Jonathan's sake? " he said one day to some members of his court.

One of them remembered hearing of an old servant of

Saul's house whose name was Ziba. David sent for Ziba, and asked him whether any of the royal house of Saul was still alive.

Perhaps Ziba was afraid to speak at first, but David said, "I want to show him kindness even as God has been kind to me." Then Ziba told the King all about Mephibosheth, and David gave orders that he was to be brought to him at once.

When the young Prince was brought into the King's presence, he was very much afraid. He was the only possible rival to the throne, and eastern monarchs had a quick way of getting rid of rivals. Mephibosheth bowed low to the ground before David, who now occupied his father's place.

But David said to him, "Fear not; for I will surely show you kindness for Jonathan your father's sake, and will restore to you all the land of Saul your grandfather: and you shall eat bread at my table continually."

Knowing that Mephibosheth was unable to work for himself, because of his lameness, David put Ziba in charge of all the fields and other property now restored to Mephibosheth.

Ziba was to have part of the income for the support of himself and his family, and the rest was to be used so that his master could live with all the high dignity of a king's son.

In this generous and kingly manner David honoured his dear friend's memory and kept the pact that they solemnly made together at the time when Jonathan warned David, by the signal of the arrows, that he was in grave danger because of the jealousy of Saul.

A Different David

Fleeing from Saul, David escaped to Nob, which was at that time the sacred city of Israel. The Tabernacle was there, and in charge of it was Ahimelech the High Priest. It was the Sabbath Day, and no doubt David felt he would be safer from his enemies at Nob, especially on the Sabbath Day.

When Ahimelech saw David, he suspected there was something wrong, and he was afraid. "Why are you alone, and no man with you?" he asked David.

Then David told his first lie. "The King has sent me on a secret mission," he told Ahimelech, "and said I was not to let anyone know my business."

This seemed likely enough, so Ahimelech was satisfied and willing to help David. David asked him for some bread, but the priest said since it was the Sabbath Day all the bread he had was holy bread which had just been taken from off the Table of Shewbread in the Holy Place. This bread was changed every day.

David pretended that his mission was for a holy purpose and so it would be all right for him to have the bread. The High Priest then gave him five loaves of the "bread of the Presence".

Then David told another lie. He said to Ahimelech, "Have you a spear or a sword you could give me? I have not brought my sword or any other weapon, because the King's business required haste."

Ahimelech replied, "The sword of Goliath the Philistine, whom you slew, is here wrapped up in a cloth behind the sacred ephod. If you would like to take that, take it, for it is the only kind of weapon that is here." "Ah," said David. "There is none like that: give it me."

The last time David had that sword in his hand, he was trusting in God. "I come to you in the name of the Lord of hosts, the God of the armies of Israel, Whom you have defied," he had told the giant. But what a different David this is who now holds that same sword! He is not trusting in the truth this time, but in his own craftiness.

Now, it so happened that because it was the Sabbath Day, when no Israelite could walk more than a certain distance without breaking the law, there was detained in the sacred city one of the servants of Saul, a chief of the herdsmen, whose name was Doeg.

Doeg saw David go to the High Priest, and he saw Ahimelech give David the bread and the sword of Goliath. When he got back to the King's court, he told Saul all that he had seen. Saul was furious and sent for the High Priest. "Why did you conspire with David against me? Why did you give him bread and a sword? Why did you encourage him in his rebellion against me?" he shouted at the priest.

Ahimelech was astounded. "Who is as faithful amongst all your servants as David?" he exclaimed. "He is the King's son-in-law, and he was on a secret mission for the King. Do not let the King suspect us of disloyalty. We did not know that David was running away from the King's presence."

Saul refused to believe Ahimelech, and he ordered his soldiers to put Ahimelech and all the members of the priestly family to death. But the soldiers refused to lay their hands on the priests of the Lord.

So the King, angrier than ever, turned to Doeg, and said to him, "Turn you, and fall upon the priests."

Doeg was not an Israelite but an Edomite, so the priests of the God of Israel meant nothing to him. At Saul's command, Doeg and his men not only slew Ahimelech, but they also went on to Nob and slew all the priests and their families, and even all their cattle. It was a terrible thing to do, and it was this awful deed more than anything else that turned the people away from Saul. But one member of the High Priest's family managed to escape. His name was Abiathar. He fled to where David had taken up his camp, and he told David of all the terrible things that had happened.

How very sorry David was now that his deception of Ahimelech should have had such terrible consequences. "I knew it that day," he said to Abiathar, "when Doeg the Edomite was there, that he would surely tell Saul: I have caused the death of all the members of your father's house.

"Stay with me," he said to the young priest, "fear not; for he that seeks my life seeks your life; but with me you shall be safeguarded."

When David became King in place of Saul, he made Abiathar High Priest in place of Ahimelech. But he was never

Ahimelech gives Goliath's sword to David.

able to undo the harm he had caused to others by telling lies to save himself.

~~~~~~~~~~~~~~~~~~~~~~

David and Saul

In his mounting jealousy and hatred, Saul hunted and harried David from place to place. For a time David took up his headquarters in a cave with a now famous name—the Cave of Adullam.

To that cave many rallied to his banner, including members of his own family, and many who were fugitives like himself, "every one that was in distress, and every one that was in debt, and every one that was embittered, and he became their leader : and there were about four hundred men."

David became a kind of Robin Hood in parts of Palestine, and the exploits of his mixed and motley crew became known far and wide.

News was brought to Saul that David's band were moving about in the wilderness of En-gedi, and he set out with a force of three thousand picked men to capture David and his followers. David led Saul a fine chase over high rocks and wild mountain goat tracks until Saul got tired and weary of it.

One hot day David and some of his men were hiding in a large dark cave when, to their amazement, Saul himself came into the cave all alone. He had left his men in the valley below, and was seeking quiet and rest from the heat outside.

In silence they watched him lie down, cover himself up with his cloak, and fall asleep. David's men urged him to take this great chance of putting away for ever the one who was the cause of all their trials and sufferings.

But David would not do so such a thing. Saul was the father of his dear friend Jonathan, and, moreover, David could never forget that Saul was the Lord's Anointed. So David spared the life of Saul but, as Saul slept, he crept up to him, and with his sword cut off a piece of the King's robe.

When Saul awoke and was going down the hill, David called after him, "My Lord, the King?" Saul turned round, and saw David bowing himself to the ground.

"Why do you heed those who tell you I seek your life?" David called down to Saul. "Now you can see that if I had wanted to kill you, I could easily have done so. Some of my men urged me to do it, but I said I would not put out my hand against the Lord's Anointed."

And David held up the piece which he had cut from Saul's robe. "The Lord judge between me and you," he said, "but my hand shall never be against you."

Saul was greatly moved by this. "You are more righteous than I am," he said to David. "If a man finds his enemy, will he let him escape? God give you good reward for what you have done to me this day." But Saul soon forgot David's kindness, and once more set out to seize David and put him to death.

Saul's army had encamped for the night, and Saul was lying asleep surrounded by his men who were also asleep, even the King's own personal bodyguard. David and one of his captains, whose name was Abishai, crept through their ranks to where the King was lying.

Saul's spear was stuck in the ground near his head, probably to mark off the place of the King, and his water-bottle lay near his pillow too. Abishai said to David, "Let me smite Saul with his own spear. I will fix him to the ground, and not require two blows to do it either!"

David restrained Abishai, "Destroy him not, for who can put his hand on the Lord's Anointed, and be held guiltless?" he said.

"But take the spear at Saul's head," he commanded Abishai, "and the water-bottle, and let us go." They both then crept back through the sleeping soldiers, and went off to the other side of the valley.

The captain of the King's guard was called Abner. "What a brave man you are!" David shouted to him across the valley. "The King might have been dead for all you knew. See now where the spear is that stood at the King's head, and the bottle of water that lay at his pillow," and David held them up for Abner to see.

"Is that your voice, my son David?" called Saul through the morning mist.

"It is my voice, my lord, O King," David shouted back across the valley. "Why is my lord still hunting his servant? Why am I being hunted like a partridge in the mountains?"

David gives Saul's spear back to him.

"I have sinned," confessed the King. "Return, my son David, for I will no more do you harm, because my life was sacred in your eyes this day. I have played the fool, and have erred exceedingly."

Then David said, "Here is the King's spear. Let one of the young men come over and fetch it. May God reward every man according to his deeds. I could have slain you this day, but I refused to put out my hand against the Lord's Anointed. As I valued your life, may the Lord value mine, and deliver me out of all my distresses."

Then Saul said to David, "Blessed be thou, my son David: you shall do great things and shall still prevail."

The Thrice-anointed King

Saul never persecuted David again, but his strange madness increased, and his skill as a soldier, though not his courage, deserted him. A great battle with the Philistines was fought on Mount Gilboa. The Israelites suffered a heavy defeat, and Saul and his three eldest sons together with many of his captains and men were slain.

David wrote a lament for Saul and Jonathan which will never be forgotten so long as good writing is treasured.

The beauty of Israel is slain upon thy high places: how are the mighty fallen.

. . . Saul and Jonathan were lovely and pleasant in their lives, and in their death they were not divided: they were swifter than eagles, they were stronger than lions.

. . . How were the mighty fallen in the midst of battle! O Jonathan, thou wert slain in thy high places.

I am distressed for thee, my brother Jonathan, very pleasant hast thou been unto me: thy love to me was wonderful, passing the love of women. How are the mighty fallen, and the weapons of war perished!

The time had now come for David to take up the high position which God had not only promised to give him, but for which God had been preparing him through many strange experiences.

David was actually anointed King three times. The first time was when, as a boy, he was anointed by the prophet Samuel. The second time was when, after the death of Saul, he was anointed King of Judah only.

Judah was the leading tribe of Israel, and they lost no time in making David their King, for he was one of themselves.

But there was one of the sons of Saul still alive, and Abner, who had been one of Saul's chief officers, made this son, whose name was Ish-bosheth, King of all the other tribes.

The reign of Ish-bosheth, however, was not popular, and

after seven and a half years he was treacherously murdered by two men who thought that by this deed they could curry favour with David. David was afterwards to put them to death for their cruel deed.

The leading men of all the tribes of Israel then came to Hebron, which was David's capital in Judah, and there David was anointed for the third time; this time, King over all the people of Israel.

Hebron, a sacred place to all Israelites because Abraham had lived there, was not a suitable place to be the capital city of Israel. There was another city which was much more fitting, Jebus, the city of the Jebusites.

It was built on high hills, and on the loftiest part was a strong citadel which the Jebusites thought to be impregnable. "The blind and the halt will prevent you," they said mockingly to David, meaning that it was so strong that blind and maimed people were sufficient to defend it.

But they did not know David. He led his men up the steep rocks, and captured the citadel, and called it "Zion, the City of David". This is the city we now know as Jerusalem, which throughout the ages has remained a very special place in the hearts of the Jewish people.

With Zion as his centre, David completed the conquest of all Canaan. And David prospered and became a great King, and he was blessed by God in all that he did. Under his wise and brave leadership, the twelve tribes of Israel were finally welded into one nation, and Israel became one of the greatest countries in the world.

Perhaps we should not hesitate to say the greatest, for although Palestine is one of the smallest countries in the world, no other country has had the same influence on all the others.

With David, God's promise to Abraham, Isaac and Jacob that their children would possess the land of Canaan was at last completely fulfilled.

The Ark of the Covenant

During all their wanderings in the wilderness, and throughout all their conquests in Canaan, the sacred Ark of the Covenant had always gone before the Children of Israel. To them it was the visible proof that God, Whom no human eye can see, was truly with them.

When the Ark was captured by the Philistines, all who sincerely loved God said, " The glory is departed from Israel, for the Ark of the Lord is taken."

The Philistines did not keep the Ark long, for it caused them nothing but plague and trouble so long as they held it in captivity. So they placed it on a newly made cart drawn by two beautiful milch-cows, and allowed the cows to wander at will in the direction of the nearest Israelite village.

The wise animals took the road straight to Bethshemesh. The men of that place rejoiced to see the Ark again, and arranged for it to be sent on to Kirjath-jearim.

There it was placed in the house of a man called Abinadab, and his son Eleazar was appointed to take care of the Ark, and there it remained for a long time.

Once he was securely seated on his throne in his new city of Jerusalem, David felt that the Ark should be in the Capital, and ordered it to be brought from Kirjath-jearim. Again it was placed on a new cart, in the charge of Abinadab's two sons, Uzza and Ahio, and guarded by thirty thousand picked men.

On the way, a very sad thing happened. The cart gave a lurch, and Uzza, thinking the Ark might tumble off, put out his hand to steady it. Uzza fell to the ground dead. It was wrong for anyone who was not a Levite to touch the sacred Ark.

This happened near the house of a man called Obed-edom. David ordered that the Ark should be carried by its two gold staves into the house, for he was now afraid to take it any farther.

God blessed the house of Obed-edom, and David saw God

was no longer displeased. After three months, David brought the Ark to Jerusalem. He went with it himself, taking the lead in the religious ceremonies and great rejoicings with which the Ark was brought from Obed-edom to Jerusalem.

David was a King without a palace, for the Israelites, who had lived so long in tents, had not yet learned how to make large buildings. But they had learned to trade with other countries, especially with the seafaring Phoenicians of Tyre.

Hiram, the King of Tyre, sent a large gift of special kinds of woods to make a palace for David, and he sent masons and carpenters to build it.

A magnificent palace was built, but David was not happy living in it. "Lo, I dwell in an house of cedars," he said, "but the Ark of the Covenant of the Lord is still in a tent."

Samuel had long since died; and in his place was Nathan the prophet. David told Nathan he would like to build a Temple for God, far greater and grander than any earthly king's palace; a permanent place where the people could worship God, as they had done in the Tabernacle in the Wilderness.

At first Nathan encouraged David to go on with such a splendid plan, but that same night God said to Nathan that David was not the one to do it.

"You shall not build a house for my name," God told David, "because you have been a man of war, and have shed blood . . . Solomon your son shall build my house and my courts."

Although David was not allowed to build the Temple, he was given the privilege and great joy of planning the Temple and of preparing the materials needed so that Solomon could go on with the building as soon as he succeeded to the throne of Israel.

David gave vast treasures out of his own treasury, and all the people gave gifts from their own property. The people were joyful and gave willingly, because they were making an offering to God.

This was history repeating itself, for the same thing had happened when Moses built the Tabernacle in the Wilderness.

Indeed the Temple which David planned and Solomon finished, followed the same pattern as that of the Tabernacle.

As in the Tabernacle, so in the Temple : there was the Holy of Holies to which, at long last, came the Ark of the Covenant with its golden cherubim whose wings reached over the golden Mercy Seat.

David's Great Sin

Bible stories of great men do not hide their faults. Great hero though David was, the Bible tells us of the great sin which cast a dark shadow over the rest of his life.

The buildings in the East usually have flat roofs, so that in hot weather the people sleep on the house-tops to keep cool.

One evening, David saw from his palace roof a beautiful woman called Bathsheba, and he fell deeply in love with her. But she was already the wife of another man called Uriah, one of David's principal soldiers.

At that time, the Israelites were at war with the Ammonites, and were besieging their city of Rabbah. The commander-in-chief was Joab, a nephew of David, and a great military leader. Uriah was one of his officers.

David sent a secret order to Joab to stage an attack upon Rabbah, and to place Uriah in a position where he was most likely to be killed by the enemy. Joab carried out this cruel order and when Uriah died, David married Bathsheba.

Such a wicked thing was common enough in those far-off times, but the thing that David had done was evil in the eyes of God.

Nathan, the prophet, came to David and told him the sad story of a poor man who had only one little ewe lamb of which he was so fond that it had become a family pet. The children loved it too. A rich man who stayed near by had a visitor come to stay with him, and, instead of taking a lamb out of his own flock, he took the poor man's only lamb to make a meal for the visitor.

David was so angry when he heard this story that he declared he would punish such a man with death, and demanded to know who the rich man was. Nathan pointed at David, and said solemnly, "You are the man!"

In this way, God made David realize how wicked was the thing he had done, and that because he had so used the sword, then the sword would cause great suffering and sorrow in his own family. A later story shows how very true this was to be.

David now saw how wicked he had been, and was very, very sorry. How sorry he was, we can see from Psalm 51 which he wrote at that time. Here are a few verses from it:

> Have mercy upon me, O God, according to thy loving kindness; according unto the multitude of thy tender mercies blot out my transgressions.
> Wash me thoroughly from my iniquities, and cleanse me from my sin.
> Purge me with hyssop, and I shall be clean: wash me, and I shall be whiter than snow.
> Create in me a clean heart, O God, and renew a right spirit within me.

The Bible makes no excuses for David, nor must we; but we should remember that he lived three thousand years ago, when an oriental king would not even think of being sorry for acting like this.

But David was so sorry that it broke his heart, and humbled him. Some of the other psalms which he wrote at this time are also expressions of his sadness and penitence.

The Foolish Prince

David's sin speedily brought shame and sadness into his own family circle. The first serious trouble started between David's two eldest sons, Ammon and Absalom. Absalom hated Ammon because he was the eldest and therefore possible heir to the throne, and also because Ammon had heaped insult on Absalom's family pride.

Absalom plotted to kill Ammon in a deliberate and cun-

Absalom rides at the head of a splendid procession.

ning manner. For two long years he waited until Ammon felt the matter between them had been forgotten. Then Absalom invited all the king's sons to a sheep-shearing feast on his own estate about ten miles from Jerusalem.

He had carefully instructed some of his servants that when Ammon had been made careless with the food, wine, and general merriment of the feast, they were to stab him with a sword.

When David heard of this wicked crime, he was overwhelmed with grief, for Ammon was his eldest son, and Absalom his favourite son.

Absalom was a handsome-looking prince. He had inherited the beauty of his father when David was a youth. One outstanding thing about Absalom was his lovely hair, which fell down over his shoulders in long, heavy tresses.

No wonder David loved Absalom, but so great was his grief over Absalom's wicked crime that he refused to see him, and Absalom fled to his uncle, the King of Geshur.

After three years, David longed to see Absalom again, and a meeting between them was arranged by Joab, Absalom's cousin. No sooner had Absalom been restored to favour, however, than he began his plotting again, and this time against David himself.

He began what, for the Israelites, was a new idea. He formed royal processions of chariots and soldiers with himself at the head. He began whispering to this man and that man that he could do better for them than the King could do. And so gradually he "stole away the hearts of the men of Israel".

When he thought the time was ripe, Absalom fled to Hebron, the old capital of Judah, and a strong army rallied to his standard.

David was now an old man, but he showed his true greatness. He was no longer a bloodthirsty man, but one of peace. He decided to leave Jerusalem lest Absalom should think of attacking and destroying it.

A large number of people remained loyal to David and went with him, including the priests, who brought with them the Ark of the Covenant.

But David sent them back. "Carry back the Ark of God into the City," he said to the priests, "if I shall find favour in the eyes of the Lord, he will bring me again, and show me both it and His holy place. But if he says, I have no delight in you; behold here am I, let him do as seems good to him."

Then David went on his way by the ascent of Mount Olivet. He was weeping as he went up, and barefooted.

When he came to the top of the mount, he worshipped God.

In this way, David showed how truly he had repented of the sin that had caused all this sorrow and suffering, and how patient and humble he had become.

~~~~~~

The Death of Absalom

When it was clear beyond all doubt that Absalom really intended to give battle to his father, David's military skill asserted itself again. He divided his loyal forces into three parts under the command of the three best generals in Israel —Joab, Abishai, and Ittai.

David wanted to lead the combined force himself, but his soldiers would not hear of it. They said that by staying in the town, which was his headquarters, to direct and encourage them, he would be worth to them more than ten thousand troops would be on the field.

So the three armies marched out before David. As the three generals went past the King, he commanded each of them in turn, "Deal gently, for my sake, with the young man, Absalom." Soon the whole army knew that this was the King's wish.

Then followed a terrible battle which raged over the whole countryside. Over twenty thousand men fell in the fight. A dense forest formed part of the battlefield. Absalom was riding through this, his long thick hair waving in the wind.

It was his lovely tresses, of which he was so proud, that were to be his undoing. For, as he rode under an oak tree, his hair was caught in the branches, and he was left hanging in the air when his mule swept on from under him.

Just then one of David's men saw him, and reported to Joab, "Behold, I saw Absalom hanging in an oak." "When you saw him like that," exclaimed Joab, "why didn't you take the chance to smite him there to the ground?"

The man replied, "I wouldn't have done such a thing for all the wealth in the world, for in our hearing the King charged you, and Abishai, and Ittai, saying, 'Beware none touch the young man'."

But Joab was not going to miss such an opportunity of getting rid of one who would be a menace to Israel so long as he lived. He took three darts in his hand, and thrust them through the heart of Absalom.

David was sitting all this while at the gate of the little town waiting for news of the battle. A watchman was stationed on the top of the wall to watch the long road leading to the town. Suddenly, he saw one man running towards the town; and then another coming in the distance a long way behind.

The first messenger to reach the King called out, "All is well; all the enemies of the King have been scattered."

But David said, "Is the young man Absalom well?" The messenger was afraid to tell the truth, so he pretended he could not really say.

The second messenger drew near. To him also David said, "Is the young man Absalom safe?" This messenger replied, "May all the king's enemies, and all who would cause him hurt, be as that young man is."

Then David felt as if his heart would break. He went up to his own private room, and broke out into pitiful crying as he went: "O my son Absalom! my son, my son, would God I had died for thee, O Absalom, my son, my son!"

The First Three

There was something about David which made men ready to die for him. In the early days, there was a band of thirty such men each of whom had done some brave deed which was long remembered in Israel.

Of that band of thirty there were three who had the proud distinction of being known as "the first three". Their names were Adino, Eleazar, and Shammah. Each had secured his place in "the first three" by an act of outstanding courage, and now together they were to do a deed of such daring that it is remembered to this very day.

It happened while David still had his headquarters in the Cave of Adullam, and was being pursued by Saul. At that

David refuses the water brought by his brave men.

time Bethlehem, David's native town, was in the hands of the Philistines.

One night, David had a great longing to see his old home. In Palestine at that time, because water was so precious, the village well was always regarded as an important landmark. David thought of the well at Bethlehem with loving recollection. Many a time he had watered his sheep there, and had taken a long, cool drink there himself.

"Oh, that someone would give me a drink of the water of the well of Bethlehem, which is by the gate!" he sighed aloud. It was like asking for the moon, for David knew that a strong garrison of Philistines was in Bethlehem.

But Adino, Eleazer, and Shammah had heard their beloved leader sigh for that water, and they determined amongst themselves that he should have it, come what might.

One night, without telling anyone, these three brave men slipped out of the camp and made their way to Bethlehem. They fought their way to the well, drew a flask of water, and fought their way back again.

When they brought the water to David, he did a strange thing with it: " he poured it out unto the Lord." That is to say, he made a drink-offering of it to God, which was one of the ways the Children of Israel worshipped God, by offering to Him something they regarded as very rare and very precious.

"Be it far from me," David said, "that I should drink this water: is not this the blood of men that went in jeopardy of their lives?" Therefore he would not drink it.

David felt that this water which had been got at such great cost was too precious to keep for himself: only God was worthy of such a priceless gift.

~~~~~~~~~~~~~~~~~~~~~~~~~~~~~~~~~~~

The Glory of Solomon

David had, after many battles, extended the Kingdom of Israel to its utmost bounds, and made it one of the great countries of the world.

What was needed now was a time of peace to establish all that had been won, and the reign of Solomon was to be the most peaceful and prosperous Israel was ever to know.

David set the course for this by urging Solomon to set his heart always to honour and serve God. The first step in this direction was to be the building of the great Temple for which David himself had long planned and prepared. Those preparations had been on a colossal scale, for the Temple was to be exceedingly magnificent, famous and glorious throughout all countries.

"Now, my son," David said to Solomon, "the Lord be with you, so that you may prosper and build the house of the Lord your God, as he has said concerning you. The Lord give you wisdom and understanding when you are King of Israel so that you may keep the law of the Lord your God.

"Then you shall prosper, if you take care to carry out all the laws and commandments the Lord gave to Moses for the children of Israel. Be strong and of good courage, do not be afraid or dismayed."

Solomon was still very young to be King over the people of God, but when the time came he remembered his father's advice, and prayed for that which would help him best in his high position. One night he had a dream. He dreamt he heard God say to him, "Ask what I shall give thee."

Solomon, in his dream, replied, "Give your servant an understanding heart to judge your people, that I may discern between good and bad : for who is able to judge this great people?"

God was very pleased that Solomon should ask for this and not for something to spend on himself. And God said unto him, "Because you have asked this thing, and have not asked for yourself long life, or riches for yourself, or the life of your enemies, but have asked for yourself understanding to judge people and things properly; behold, I have done according to your prayer : I have given you a wise and understanding heart; so that there was none like you in the past and there shall be none like you in the future. And I have also given you that for which you did not ask, both riches and honour; so that there shall not be another king like you all your days."

The Queen of Sheba was one of the many great persons who came to see the splendour of Solomon's court. "It was a true report that I heard in my own land of your acts and of your wisdom," she said to Solomon. "But I could not believe the report until I came and saw it with my own eyes;

and what I heard was not half of what I have seen. Your wisdom and your prosperity exceed the fame of it."

Solomon has been called the wisest man who ever lived, and certainly, so long as he remembered to honour God, he

The Queen of Sheba visits Solomon.

was very wise. His grandeur and glory were even greater; so great, indeed, that when the Lord Jesus wanted to show how God cares for all His creatures He said, "Consider the lilies of the field; how they grow; they toil not, neither do they spin: And yet I say unto you, that even Solomon in all his glory was not arrayed like one of these."

The Building of the Temple

Perhaps the greatest thing in the history of the Jewish people was the Temple in Jerusalem. There were three such Temples altogether, built one after the other on the top of Mount Moriah, on the exact spot where Abraham was ready to sacrifice Isaac. To-day the site is occupied by a Mohammedan mosque.

The first of the three temples is usually called Solomon's Temple, but it might just as truly be called David's Temple. It was David who dreamed of it first, and who largely planned it, and prepared the materials for it. But it was Solomon who built the Temple, and the story of its building is a very interesting one.

The Temple was built mainly of cedar wood, stone, and much silver and gold. The cedar trees grew far away to the north, on the mountain slopes of Lebanon. David's old friend, Hiram, King of Tyre and Sidon, owned the cedar forests.

The Sidonians were then the most famous lumbermen in the world. Hiram's men cut down the cedar trees, and the huge logs were then lashed together to form great rafts, and floated down the coast to the nearest port to Jerusalem.

The huge stones were cut out of the mountain quarries. They were dressed by the stone-masons at the quarries before they were carried to Mount Moriah, "so that neither hammer, nor axe, nor any tool of iron was heard in the house while it was building".

Hundreds of thousands of men were employed in the work, most of them being made to do it whether they wanted to or not. This was to have serious consequences later on. It is never right to force innocent people to work against their will, especially when the work is for God.

The Temple was really one of several large buildings, enclosed in three courts—the large court, the middle court, and the inner court, where the Temple was, and all were surrounded by a high wall.

The Temple itself was built after the style of the old Tabernacle, and was about twice as large. Like the Tabernacle, it had two main parts—the outer room called the Holy Place, and the inner room called the Holy of Holies. But there was also a kind of entrance hall, or vestibule, which had a high porch. The huge pillars on either side of this porch have an interesting story.

Hiram, the Phoenician King, sent to Solomon skilled workers in wood, stone, gold, silver, and bronze. Amongst them was a very clever worker in bronze whose name, strangely enough, was also Hiram. This Hiram made many wonderful bronze vessels and articles, including the two bronze pillars for the porch. These were nearly forty feet high and twenty feet round. They were joined at the top by a beautifully decorated bronze curtain or frieze. The Temple, indeed, must have been not unlike some Churches that may be seen in our own land.

These two pillars had two strange names: one was called Jachin, which means "established", and the other was called Boaz, which means "strength". So the whole porch spoke to all who saw it of the sure foundation of faith in God.

It took more than seven years to build the Temple. When all was ready, the Ark of the Covenant was placed in the Holy of Holies, and all the other furniture of the old Tabernacle was placed in the Holy Place; or at least the new and more elaborate versions of them made by Solomon.

Then came the great day of Dedication. Solomon offered a very beautiful prayer:

But will God indeed dwell on the earth? Behold, the heaven and heaven of heavens cannot contain thee; how much less this house that I have builded?

Yet have thou respect unto the prayer of thy servant, and to his supplication, O Lord my God, to hearken unto the cry and to the prayer which thy servant prayeth before thee to-day:

That thine eyes may be open toward this house night and day, even toward the place of which thou hast said, My name shall be there; that thou mayest hearken unto the prayer which thy servant shall make toward this place.

And hearken thou to the supplication of thy servant, and of thy people Israel, when they pray toward this place; and hear thou in heaven thy dwelling place; and when thou hearest, forgive.

Solomon was really asking God that the Temple might be like an anchor to the Children of Israel when the storms of adversity came upon them; and, in times of prosperity, a constant reminder to them that God is the giver of every good and perfect gift.

The festival of dedication lasted twice seven days, and then Solomon sent the people home. "And they blessed the King, and went to their tents joyful and glad of heart for all the goodness that the Lord had done for David his servant, and for Israel his people."

Thus David's great desire was fulfilled. The Temple was to mean even more to his people throughout their long and varied history than ever he had dreamed it could be.

But God was to teach His people, by the prophets and messengers He sent to them, that the time would come when earthly temples would be no more. In the very last Book of the Bible, the Apostle John tells us of the great vision he had of the Holy City, New Jerusalem, coming down from God out of heaven, and he says that the city had no temple for God was in it, and there was no need of sun or moon because it was lit by the glory of God.

The Prophet and the Ravens

The glory of Solomon had a darker side to it. The colossal expense of it all bore heavily on the people, especially the poorer people. For those who could not pay the heavy taxes in money were compelled to pay in forced labour.

When Solomon died, the leaders of the ten Northern tribes came to Rehoboam, his son, and said to him, "Your father made our life hard: now, therefore, make the grievous service of your father, and the heavy burden which he placed upon us, lighter, and we will serve you."

Rehoboam had, unfortunately, inherited nothing of his father's wisdom. He had surrounded himself with counsellors as young and foolish as himself. The older counsellors advised caution, but the young men told Rehoboam what to say to the men from the north.

"My father made your yoke heavy," he told them, "and I will add to your hardship: my father chastised you with whips, but I will chastise you with scorpions."

When they heard this, the leaders of the ten tribes replied, "What had David to do with us? We have no interest in his heirs or inheritance. To your tents, O Israel!"

So the nation was divided into two again—the tribes of Judah and Benjamin in the south; the remaining ten tribes in the north. It was never to be the same whole nation again.

Jeroboam, who before had led a rebellion against Solomon and then fled to Egypt, was brought back, and made King of the Northern Kingdom. In some ways he was a clever leader, but he did one very bad thing: he set up a form of idol-worship along with the worship of the true God, which was quite contrary to the commandment not to make graven images, which command God had given them through Moses.

Some years later, another King did the same. His name was Ahab. But Ahab did something even worse. He married a very wicked woman from a foreign country. Her name was Jezebel.

Jezebel brought with her an idol called Baal and four hundred and fifty priests of Baal to teach the people of Israel this false religion, and to forget the worship of the only true God.

But at this point God sent one of his prophets—the first of a great succession of prophets, and one of the greatest of them all. His name was Elijah.

106

Elijah, who came from Tishbite in Gilead, is first heard of when he went to Ahab to warn him that, because he had consented to the wickedness of Jezebel, there was going to be a drought. He said: "As the Lord God of Israel lives,

The widow bakes a scone for Elijah.

before whom I stand, there shall not be any rain or dew, except as I say."

Lack of water is a serious matter anywhere, and especially so in a hot climate, for there everything dries up almost immediately. Famine and plague quickly follow. This was

107

the sore punishment Ahab had brought upon his people by his wickedness.

Elijah had to hide himself, because of the anger of Ahab who blamed him for this terrible disaster. God told Elijah to hide himself amongst the hills by the lonely brook Cherith which was in the eastern part of the country near Jordan.

Elijah had water to drink, but what about food which was now so scarce? "I have commanded the ravens to feed you," God said to him. And the ravens brought him bread and meat in the morning, and bread and meat in the evening.

There he lived for many days, safe from Ahab, and fed every day by God's faithful little messengers from the air.

The Widow of Sarepta

So long and severe was the drought that even the brook Cherith dried up. But God had other plans for His servant the prophet.

God told Elijah to go to Sarepta, a city in the district of Zidon, which was not in Israel at all, and to live there in the house of a widow who would give him food and lodging.

When Elijah came near to Sarepta, he saw a woman gathering sticks near the city gate. He asked her for a drink of water. As she was going for the water, Elijah called after her, "And bring me, I pray you, a little bit of bread." These two things were the scarcest things in the whole land.

"Alas," said the woman, "I have no bread, only a handful of meal; that and a little olive oil is all the food I have in the house.

"I am gathering a few sticks for a fire on which to bake a scone for myself and my son. Then," she continued pitifully, "after that we must die, for there is nothing else left to eat."

She mentioned only herself and her son, so Elijah guessed
108

this was the widow of whom God had told him. "Don't be afraid," he said to her; "go on with your baking, but bake me a little scone first, and bring it to me, and then bake more for yourself and your son."

The woman looked at the prophet in amazement, but Elijah had something more to say to her. "God has promised," he said, "that the barrel of meal shall not diminish nor the cruse of oil fail until he sends rain upon the earth again."

The woman trusted the word of God through His prophet, and her faith was rewarded. She baked the scone for Elijah, and from that moment there was always meal in the meal-barrel and oil in the oil-vessel, so long as the famine lasted.

For more than a year Elijah lived in Sarepta in the home of the widow and her son. One day the boy became very ill and died. His mother went in great distress to the prophet and told him that his coming to her home was not a good thing after all. He was a holy man, and because he had found out she was a sinful woman, he had brought this punishment upon her.

But Elijah took the boy and carried him up to his own room. He laid the boy on his bed, and then prayed to God. He asked God so to over-rule this happening that the poor woman would have no reason to think she was being punished for being kind to a prophet of God.

Elijah then pressed his heart to the little boy's heart, and prayed again, "O Lord my God, I pray thee, let this child's spirit come back to him again." God answered Elijah's prayer, and gradually the little boy revived. Taking the child in his arms, Elijah brought him down to where his mother was anxiously waiting, and said to her, "See, thy son lives!"

And the woman said to Elijah, "Now by this I do know you are a man of God and that what you say is indeed the word of God."

This woman of Sarepta is mentioned in the New Testament by our Lord Himself. He told the people in His own town of Nazareth who were refusing to believe in Him, "Verily I say unto you, No prophet is honoured in his own country.

But I tell you of a truth, many widows were in Israel in the days of Elijah, when the heaven was shut up three years and six months, when great famine was throughout the land. But to none of them was Elijah sent, save unto Sarepta, a city of Zidon, unto a woman that was a widow."

Thus a widow's faith was remembered a thousand years after to rebuke those who had no faith.

On Mount Carmel

The drought and famine lasted more than three years. At the end of that time, God said to Elijah, "Go, show yourself to Ahab and I will send rain upon the earth." When Ahab saw Elijah he said to him, "Are you the man who troubles Israel?"

"It is not I who has troubled Israel, but you," replied Elijah, "in that you have forsaken the commandments of the Lord, and have followed Baal."

Elijah told Ahab that the day of final reckoning had come, and commanded him in the name of God to call together the people of Israel to Mount Carmel, and to gather also the four hundred and fifty priests of Baal which Jezebel had brought into the land.

When all this great throng of people and priests had been gathered together, Elijah cried out to the people, "How long will you halt between two opinions? If the Lord be God, follow him : but if Baal, then follow him." There was dead silence over the vast crowd.

Then Elijah said, "I am the only one that remains of all the prophets of the Lord; but Baal has four hundred and fifty," and he proposed a test to prove which were the true prophets of the true God.

He proposed that Baal's priests should prepare a sacrifice of a bullock, and that he would do the same. The bullocks were to be dressed ready for the sacrifice and put upon wood, but no fire was to be put under the wood.

Then the priests of Baal were to call upon their god, and Elijah would call upon the name of the Lord, and, said Elijah, let this be the test, "The God that answers by fire, let him be God." All the people answered, "It is well spoken."

Elijah told the priests of Baal that they should have the first chance since they were so many. The priests of Baal made their sacrifice ready and then called on Baal from morning till noon, chanting incessantly "O Baal, hear us! O Baal, hear us!"

But there was no answer, and the priests of Baal kept dancing and leaping up and down, round and round the altar, chanting all the time.

As the fiery eastern sun reached its full strength at noon, Elijah began to mock the priests of Baal. "Cry louder!" he said to them. "Your Baal is a god, you say. Perhaps he is talking to someone and can't hear you. Perhaps he is hunting, or away on a long journey. Perhaps he's sleeping, and you'll have to wake him. Cry louder!"

And the priests of Baal got more and more excited. They leaped and danced, and shouted and pleaded. They cut themselves with knives, as Dervishes still do in the East when they have worked themselves up into a frenzy. But nothing happened. As evening drew on, their sacrifice remained black and cold.

Then Elijah told the people to come near. He took twelve stones, one to represent each of the twelve tribes of Israel, and with those stones he built an altar. Round about the altar he dug a deep trench.

He put the pieces of the bullock in order on the wood on the altar. He then asked for four barrels of the precious water to be poured over the sacrifice and the wood. He commanded it to be done a second time, and then a third time, until the altar was drenched with water, and the trench filled to overflowing.

Then Elijah prayed, "Lord God of Abraham, Isaac, and of Israel, let it be known this day that thou art God in Israel, and that I am thy servant, and that I have done all these things at thy word."

Then the fire of the Lord fell, and consumed the burnt sacrifice, and the wood and the stones and the dust, and licked up the water that was in the trench. When the people saw this amazing sight, they fell on their faces and cried, "The Lord, he is the God."

Elijah was quick to seize this great chance of wiping out the idolatry of Baal, and he ordered the people to seize the priests of Baal, and to slay them all by the brook Kishon; which they did.

And Elijah said to Ahab, "Get up, eat and drink, for there is a sound of abundance of rain."

When Ahab went away, Elijah went to the top of Mount Carmel, bowed himself to the ground, and prayed that the rain might now come upon the parched land. As he prayed, he told his servant to look towards the Mediterranean Sea, away in the distance, and to tell what he could see. The servant replied, "There is nothing."

Elijah told him seven times to go and look towards the sea, and on the seventh time, the servant called out, "Behold, there is a small cloud rising up out of the sea, like a man's hand."

Elijah knew that was the answer at last. "Go up," he said to his servant, "and say to Ahab, prepare your chariot, and get you down, before the rain stops you."

Then the sky, which had been like brass for more than three years, became black with clouds, and a rainstorm broke upon the thirsty land.

Through that storm of rain rode Ahab in his chariot, towards the city of Jezreel. But swifter than Ahab's horses ran the prophet Elijah, for the power of God so came upon that strange man that he sped those twenty miles through the rain his prayers had caused, and when Ahab reached the city at last, Elijah was there to meet him.

The Still, Small Voice

Queen Jezebel was furious when she heard what had happened to her prophets. She sent a messenger to Elijah threatening him with her cruel vengeance. "So let the gods do to me, and more, if I do not do to you within twenty-four hours what you did to the priests of Baal."

It says much for the kind of woman that Jezebel was that when Elijah the prophet received this message, he felt it would be best for him to get as far away from her as he possibly could.

So he made first for Beersheba, which is in Judah. Even there he did not feel safe, so he went a day's journey further into the wilderness, and sat down under a juniper tree.

What was really wrong with Elijah was not cowardice but sheer physical weakness. The thrilling happenings on Mount Carmel had been a great strain on him, and he had not eaten food for some days. Moreover, he felt he had failed to to do his task properly, and this depressed him. He felt, too, that he was the only one left to maintain the true faith, and that if he died, it would die too. Ever since then a juniper tree has been regarded as the symbol of sadness.

Elijah fell asleep under the juniper tree, and had a strange dream. He dreamt an angel touched him and said to him, " Arise and eat."

When he looked, he saw a scone baking on the fire and a bottle of water at his pillow. So he ate and drank, and then fell asleep again; but not for very long.

The same thing happened again. " Arise and eat: because the journey is too great for you," said the angel. Elijah did eat and drink, and went in the strength of that heavenly food " forty days and forty nights"—a term in the Scriptures which usually means " a very long time ".

Elijah continued his journey to Mount Horeb—also known as Mount Sinai. This was the sacred mount of God on which Moses had seen the Burning Bush, and from which he later received the Commandments from God; no doubt, Elijah felt that here, if anywhere, he would learn what God wanted him to do.

When he got to Mount Horeb, Elijah lodged in a cave, and there he heard the voice of God speak to him. "What are you doing here, Elijah?" the Voice said to him.

"I have been very daring for the Lord God of Hosts," said Elijah. "The Children of Israel have forsaken thy covenant,

After the earthquake, Elijah sees the fire but still hears no voice.

thrown down thine altars, and slain thy prophets with the sword : and I, even I only, am left : and they are trying to kill me too."

"Go outside the cave," answered the Voice, "and stand before the Lord." Then a very strange thing happened. A terrible gale of wind blew over the mountains, as if breaking them in pieces. Elijah listened for the Voice to speak in the gale, but he heard no Voice.

Then a great earthquake shook Mount Horeb, but still there was no Voice. A flame of fire then played about the Mount, but still no Voice.

After the fire had passed, Elijah heard a calm, quiet Voice, and he hid his face in his cloak, just as Moses had done before the Burning Bush, for he knew that it was the Voice of God that was speaking to him.

"What are you doing here, Elijah?" the Voice said again. And once more Elijah gave the same reason for his despair and anxiety.

But the quiet Voice said to him, "Go back again, for I have seven thousand left in Israel, who have not bowed the knee to Baal or shown any love for his worship."

So Elijah returned to Israel, greatly comforted that he was not alone, for there was a great company of men and women still loyal to God, in spite of Jezebel. Better still, he had the assurance of that still, small Voice that God was with him too.

The Chariot of Fire

One of the brave seven thousand who had not worshipped Jezebel's Baal was a young farmer called Elisha.

One day Elisha was ploughing in his father's fields. He had twelve yoke of oxen, which shows that his father must have been a prosperous farmer. In the distance, Elisha saw a strange figure coming towards him. As the figure drew nearer, Elisha saw that it was the great prophet of Israel, Elijah.

As Elijah passed along the long team of oxen and came to where Elisha was, he took his mantle, or cloak, and cast it over Elisha. Elisha knew at once what that meant, and he obeyed the sign and call.

Elisha ran after Elijah and said to him, "Let me, I pray you, say good-bye to my father and mother, and then I will follow you." Elijah looked upon the young man, and said very tenderly, "Go back again, for what have I done to you?" Elijah knew how hard and difficult the life of a prophet could be.

But Elisha was determined to obey the call, and his parents seemed to have been willing too, for a great feast was given to all the folk on the farm to mark the great occasion. Then Elisha left his home and people to become Elijah's servant.

We do not know how long Elisha was the servant of Elijah, but it is clear from the Scriptures that he greatly loved the brave old prophet, and looked upon him as a father. We also know that Elijah was sure that this was the man who would carry on after himself the great work of restoring the true faith amongst the people of Israel.

The day came when Elijah realized his work was finished and that God was about to take him away. He tried to spare his young servant the pain of parting, but Elisha refused to leave his beloved master, for he too knew the time was drawing near when he would see Elijah no more.

When the dreaded day came, Elijah said to Elisha, "Ask what I shall do for you, before I am taken away from you." Elisha replied, "I pray you, let me inherit your spirit."

"You have asked a hard thing," Elijah said, "nevertheless, if you see me when I am being taken from you, it shall be so unto you; but if not, it shall not be so."

Elisha was indeed with Elijah when the prophet was taken from him, and it was a very strange way in which he saw Elijah go. As they were going along talking together, suddenly a vision of a chariot of fire drawn by horses of fire came between them, like the wind of a whirlwind, and when the vision was gone Elijah was gone too, and Elisha saw him no more.

Elisha's eyes followed the chariot and horses of fire until they vanished into the heavens. "My father, my father!" he cried, "the chariot of Israel and the horsemen thereof." Elisha felt that, with the going of Elijah, Israel had lost its greatest strength and defence—greater than all the armies and chariots of war put together.

As Elisha looked, he saw that the mantle of the prophet had fallen from him. He picked it up and returned to the nearby city of Jericho. When the sons of the prophets who were there saw him, they said, " The spirit of Elijah rests on Elisha," and from that moment Elisha was recognized as the prophet of God in Elijah's place by all the people of Israel.

The Little Slave-Girl

Syria and Israel were often at war with one another, and border raids frequently occurred between them. On one of those raids, a little girl had been captured and carried from Israel to Syria. She was given as a slave-girl to Naaman's wife.

Naaman was a great soldier and Commander-in-Chief of the Syrian armies. The King of Syria held him in great honour, because of the many victories Naaman had won for his country.

The home to which the little girl had come as a maid to its mistress was a large house full of many lovely and luxurious things she had never seen before. But she noticed that over all the household there was a feeling of sadness. She soon found out the reason for this—Naaman, the great general, was a leper.

The disease had perhaps not gone very far, but no one knew a cure for it, and Naaman, in spite of all his riches and honours, was doomed, sooner or later, to the dreaded isolation and dreadful death of the leper.

One day, the little maid said to her mistress, "Would that my master Naaman were with the prophet in Samaria, for he would heal him of his leprosy." Someone who overheard this remark must have seen more in it than Naaman's wife seems to have done, for he went and told Naaman.

Anyone who has leprosy will clutch at even the slightest

hope of a cure, and Naaman must have mentioned the matter to the King. "Get ready at once to go," said the King, "and I will send a letter to the King of Israel."

So Naaman set out for Samaria, taking with him a train of camels laden with gold, silver, and silks.

When he reached the King of Israel, he handed over the letter from his own King. The King of Israel opened the letter and this is what it said, "When this letter reaches you, it will be handed to you by Naaman, my servant. You are to cure him of his leprosy."

The King of Israel got into a terrible state. "What does he think I am?" he shouted to his courtiers. "Does he think I am God that I can cure a man of his leprosy? Don't you think this is all an excuse for a quarrel?"

Elisha was told about the King's temper, and he sent this message to him. "Why do you carry on like that? Send the man to me now; and he shall know that there is a prophet in Israel."

So, in due course, Naaman and all his magnificent retinue drew up at the door of the house where Elisha was staying. Gehazi, Elisha's servant, came out and told him, "The prophet says you are to go and wash in Jordan seven times, and your flesh will be restored to you again, and you shall be clean from leprosy."

Naaman became very angry when he heard this. "Here have I been thinking all the time I was coming to this place, that he would come out to me, stand and call on the name of the Lord his God, wave his hand over the place where the leprosy is, and cure me. Are not the rivers of Damascus better than all the waters of this dirty old Jordan?" And he stalked off in a great rage.

But some of his servants came near to him, and said, "My father, if the prophet had asked you to do some great thing, you would have done it, wouldn't you? Well, then, why not do what he asks when he just says, 'Wash and be clean'?"

Naaman saw the wisdom of that, and he went down into the river Jordan, and dipped himself seven times in the water, as the prophet had told him to do, and, sure enough, as he rose up for the seventh time, his flesh was like the flesh of a child, and he was clean from his leprosy.

Naaman and all his attendants went back to Elisha's house, and Naaman said to him, "Now I know there is no God in

Naaman bathes in the Jordan and is cured of his leprosy.

all the earth, but in Israel. Now, I pray you, let me give you a present."

But Elisha said at once, "As the Lord lives before whom I stand, I will take not a thing." Naaman went on trying to persuade Elisha to take some reward, but the prophet refused.

Then Naaman asked for a present for himself, and a very strange one it was. "Well," he said, "let your servant have two mules' burden of earth, for I will henceforth offer neither sacrifice nor worship unto any other gods, but the Lord."

In those days, men believed that each country had its own God, and that each God was confined to his own country. So he wanted to take a little bit of the land of Israel with him, so that he could worship the God of Israel on it, back home in his own land.

Naaman was learning the truth about God but only little by little, for he went on to ask another favour. "In this thing may the Lord pardon your servant: when my master goes into the house of Rimmon (which was the god of the Syrians) leaning on my arm, and I bow myself in the house of Rimmon; when I bow myself in the house of Rimmon, the Lord pardon your servant in this thing."

Elisha simply replied, "Go in peace." But since this was the usual way of saying good-bye, we are not to think that Elisha was really approving of any such thing.

The little maid is nameless, but she will never be forgotten as long as the Bible is read. Her story has thrilled boys and girls in all ages since, and all over the world: how, instead of moaning about her sad lot, she looked upon herself as a missionary, carrying the message of the true faith to a foreign land.

Daniel, Shadrach, Meshach and Abednego

The little country of Palestine has always been one of the most important countries in the world because of its geographical position. It links up the three continents of Africa, Asia and Europe. All the would-be conquerers of the world have, sooner or later, tried to capture this little country which is no bigger than Wales.

The first nation which set out to conquer the world was Assyria with its ancient city of Nineveh. Long after Elisha had passed away, the Assyrians conquered the northern country of Israel, and carried off most of its people to the far north.

The Assyrians also attempted to conquer the southern kingdom of Judah, and, although they did carry off many of the Jews also, they were finally defeated.

But not by the Jews. While they were besieging Jerusalem, God smote the Assyrians with a mysterious plague, and they fled back in terror to their own country. You may read about this in 2 Kings 19.

Another great Empire arose which conquered even the Assyrians. This was the great Babylonian Empire which included Judah within its frontiers. The Babylonians destroyed Jerusalem, and carried off most of the leading Jews into captivity in Babylon.

Amongst them were four young Jews called Daniel, Shadrach, Meshach, and Abednego. Because these belonged to princely families, they were selected for training as officials in the palace of Nebuchadnezzar, the King of Babylon. " And the King appointed them a daily provision of the King's meat, and of the wine which he drank; so nourishing them three years, that at the end of this period they might stand before the King."

Now Daniel "purposed in his heart that he would not defile himself with the portion of the King's meat, nor with the wine which he drank". As part of their training, the young men were being asked to eat food and drink wine which were contrary to the commandments of God, which Moses gave to the Jews, and they were not willing to do this. So Daniel went to Ashpenaz, the official in charge of them, and asked permission not to eat the food or drink the wine.

Ashpenaz had come to like Daniel very much, but he was afraid to grant him this request. " I am afraid what the King might do to me," he said, " if you do not take his meat and wine. If you were to look thinner and paler than the others —why! I might even lose my head."

Daniel had to think of another plan. He went to the steward who served the food and wine, and said to him, "Let us try an experiment for ten days only. Give the four of us only vegetables to eat and water to drink. Then, at the end of ten days, see for yourself whether we look healthier than the others or not."

The steward agreed to do this, and at the end of the time Daniel and his companions looked far healthier and happier than all the other young men. So the steward allowed them to continue on this simple diet.

Not only were they "fairer and fatter", as the Bible says, but they were much more clever at their lessons too. And at the end of the three years, when they stood before the King for their examination, the King found that in all matters of wisdom and understanding they were "ten times better than all the magicians and astrologers that were in his realm".

"Daniel purposed in his heart" is just another way of saying Daniel made up his mind. He decided to stand for what he believed to be the right and the true. And, as we shall see, one victory helped him to win another.

The Forgotten Dream

The great Nebuchadnezzar woke up one morning with a very curious feeling. During the night he had dreamed a dream which had troubled him then, and still troubled him. But for the life of him he could not remember what it was all about.

He felt like someone who has received a warning of something terrible about to happen but cannot remember what the warning was and so does not know what to do to prevent it. So the King sent for all the astrologers, magicians and sorcerers, and there were plenty of them, for the Babylonians believed strongly in omens and magic. Many of them, indeed, were clever men, for science and learning had made great progress in Babylon, but it was still mixed with much superstition.

When the great and weird-looking crowd stood before him, Nebuchadnezzar said, " I have dreamed a dream, and my spirit was troubled to know the meaning." The astrologers, magicians, and sorcerers jauntily replied, " O King, may you live for ever. Tell us the dream, and we will show you the meaning."

" But I have forgotten what it was," said the King. " If you can't tell me what it was and what it means, I shall cut you all up into little pieces. But if you show me my dream again, and tell me the meaning of it, I shall give you great gifts, rich rewards, and heap you with honours."

The King knew those men. On previous occasions, they had pretended to know the meanings of dreams, and, while he had his doubts, he could not prove them wrong. But he would recognize his own dream, and so he demanded this very sure proof of their ability.

The astrologers and all the others kept on saying, " Let the King tell us his dream, and we will tell him the meaning of it."

" You are only behaving like this to gain time," shouted the King at them all. " If you will not make known the dream to me, there is but one end for you all. You are good at saying things, hoping for something to turn up. Now, tell me the dream, and then I'll believe you can tell me the meaning."

The wretched men complained, " Nobody in the whole world can tell the King what he asks; and no King, however great and mighty, has ever asked such a thing before. The King is asking something too hard for us : only the gods can tell him what his dream was."

Nebuchadnezzar was very angry and ordered that all the wise men of Babylon should be put to death as impostors. Now, Daniel and his companions were regarded as wise men, according to the law and custom of Babylon, although they were not present when the King sent for the astrologers, magicians, and sorcerers.

When the Captain of the King's Guard came to arrest Daniel

and his companions, Daniel said to him, "Why is the King's decree so hasty and so severe?" When the Captain told him the whole business, Daniel asked for an audience of the King, and begged that if the King would give him time, he would show the King the meaning of his dream.

When this was granted, Daniel went home and sent for Shadrach, Meshach, and Abednego, and the four young men prayed together that God in His mercy would show them the secret of the King's dream so that they should not perish along with the rest of the wise men of Babylon.

During the night, God revealed the secret to Daniel, and Daniel gave thanks to God, "Blessed be the name of God for ever and ever : for wisdom and might are his."

Daniel hurried to the Captain of the Guard and begged him not to carry out the decree to destroy the wise men. "Bring me in before the King," he said, "and I will show the King the meaning of his dream."

The Captain hurried to the King with Daniel, and said to the King, "I have found one of the captives from Judah who will make known to the King the meaning of his dream."

Nebuchadnezzar, the mighty monarch of one of the world's great empires, looked at the young Jew, an exile in a foreign country. "Are you able to make known to me the dream which I have seen, and its meaning?" he asked.

Daniel replied, "The secret which the King has demanded to know, the wise men, the astrologers, the magicians, and the soothsayers cannot show the King. But there is a God in heaven who reveals secrets. As for me, this secret is not revealed to me because of any wisdom that I have more than any other man, but because God wants you to know the meaning of your dream, and the thoughts of your heart."

It was, indeed, a strange dream which Daniel recalled to the mind of Nebuchadnezzar. In his dream the King had seen an immense and shining statue, terrifying to look at. Its head was made of fine gold; its breast and arms of silver, the lower part of its body and the upper part of its legs were made of bronze, and the lower parts of iron; its feet were made partly of iron and partly of clay.

As Nebuchadnezzar, in his dream, looked at this strange statue, made up of so many different parts, he noticed a huge stone being hewn out of a mountain by invisible hands. This huge stone started to roll with great speed towards the giant statue and hit it with a tremendous smack on its feet of iron and clay, smashing them to pieces.

Then the whole statue fell apart; the iron, the clay, the

Nebuchadnezzar dreams about a strange statue.

bronze, the silver, and the gold pieces were broken into tiny bits, and the wind blew them all away like chaff from a threshing-floor until there was nothing left that could be seen at all.

The stone which had obliterated the huge statue in this manner, grew bigger and bigger until it filled the whole world.

This was the dream which had troubled the King and which he had forgotten until Daniel pictured it for him again. Then Daniel proceeded to tell the King what the dream meant.

125

" You, O King, are a king of kings, for the God of heaven has given you a kingdom, power, and strength, and glory. God has given everything into your hand, and you are ruler over them all. You are the head of gold.

" After you shall arise another kingdom not as great as yours. Then another, a third, which is the bronze kingdom and which shall rule over the whole earth.

"The fourth kingdom shall be strong as iron, breaking everything before it into pieces. But it shall be a divided kingdom, just as you saw that the toes on the feet were partly clay and partly iron. It will have strength in it, but it will have weakness in it too, so it shall not stand together."

Then Daniel went on to speak about the stone that had been cut out of the mountain by invisible hands. " In the days of those kings shall the God of heaven set up a kingdom which shall never be destroyed: this kingdom shall break in pieces and consume all these other kingdoms, and it shall stand for ever."

Nebuchadnezzar could now see his dream and understand it. He saw that the God Who was speaking to him through his dream was the true God over all, before Whom empires rise and pass away; Who was from the beginning and has no end. He is the God Who works out His own great purposes through all the changes of history, in all ages and in all the world. All other kingdoms will pass away, but the kingdom which God is building up will never pass away. It is of this Kingdom we are thinking when we pray, "Thy Kingdom come. Thy will be done on earth as it is in Heaven."

Nebuchadnezzar was so convinced of the truth of what Daniel had told him that he actually bowed down before Daniel as the representative of the true God. "Of a truth," he said, "your God is God of gods, and Lord of kings."

" Then the King made Daniel a great man, and gave him great gifts, and made him ruler over the whole province of Babylon, and chief of the governors over all the wise men."

Daniel did not forget his companions in his prosperity. At his request, the King appointed Shadrach, Meshach, and Abednego over the affairs of the province of Babylon.

Trial By Fire

Nebuchadnezzar very soon not only forgot his strange dream but the serious warning it was meant to bring as well. He began to feel so proud and powerful that he even felt greater than God Himself. Now he demanded that men should worship him instead of God.

He set up a colossal golden statue on the great plain of Dura in the province of Babylon. This statue was about fifty feet high and about ten feet broad. Probably it was made of wood overlaid with gold. He appointed a day for the dedication of the statue, and summoned all the princes, governors, captains, judges, treasurers, counsellors, sheriffs, and all the rulers of the land to this great dedication.

When they were all gathered before the great golden statue, a herald stepped forward and made this announcement:

"To you it is commanded, all peoples, nations, and languages, that when you hear the music of the King's musicians, you shall fall down and worship the golden image that Nebuchadnezzar has set up:

"And whoso does not fall down and worship shall the same hour be cast into the midst of a burning fiery furnace."

The great day came, and an immense crowd of people gathered on the plain of Dura. There, looking tiny in the vast distance, stood the colossal image of gold. Near the image could be seen the red smoke of the fiery furnace.

At the sound of the music, the great congregation fell flat on their faces before the image—all but three young men. Spies had been scattered throughout the crowd, and they could hardly fail to see the three solitary figures standing erect on their feet when all the rest were flat on the ground. The spies did not fail to notice something else—the three young men were Jews! They were, indeed, Shadrach, Meshach, and Abednego, the friends of Daniel.

When the matter was reported to the King, he sent for the three young captives from Jerusalem whom he had so recently appointed to high positions in Babylon. He could hardly contain himself, so great was his rage. "Is it true, O Shadrach, Meshach, and Abednego, you do not serve my gods, nor worship the golden image I have set up? Now, I shall give you one more chance," he continued grimly. "If you are ready, at the sound of the music, to fall down and worship the image I have made, well and good; but if not, you will be cast into the midst of the burning fiery furnace, and who is that God that can deliver you out of my hands?"

The three young men made a calm reply to the King. "We do not need to take long to answer you, O Nebuchadnezzar.

Shadrach, Meshach and Abednego are unhurt by the fire.

If we must be cast into the fiery furnace, our God Whom we serve is able to deliver us from it; and He will deliver us out of your hand, O King. But even if He were not to deliver us, be it known to you, O King, that we will not serve your gods, nor worship the golden image which you have set up."

Now, there is nothing that makes a tyrant so angry as to know that there is something his great power cannot do or someone whose will is stronger than his own. So Nebuchadnezzar was maddened by the quiet determination of the three young men before him.

He ordered the fiery furnace to be made seven times hotter than it was already, and he commanded the strongest men in his army to bind the three young men and to throw them into the furnace. The heat was so great that the flames shot out and burned the soldiers as they were throwing their prisoners into the fire.

From a safe distance, Nebuchadnezzar could see right into the furnace, and what he saw amazed him. "Did we not cast three men bound into the midst of the fire?" he asked his counsellors.

"True, O King," they answered him.

"Lo, I see four men loose, walking in the midst of the fire," exclaimed the astonished monarch, "and they have no hurt; and the form of the fourth is like the Son of God."

Then, going nearer the door of the furnace, Nebuchadnezzar called out, "Shadrach, Meshach, and Abednego, you who serve the most high God, come out of the fire, and come near to me."

As the three young men came from the furnace, all the princes, governors, captains, and King's counsellors gathered round them, and gazed at the men upon whom the fire had had no power. Not a hair of their heads was singed; not a sign or smell of fire even upon their clothes.

Then Nebuchadnezzar called out, "Blessed be the God of Shadrach, Meshach, and Abednego Who has sent His angel, and delivered His servants that trusted in Him. These men made the word of a King of no effect, because they were willing to yield their bodies to the flame rather than serve and worship any god except their own God.

"Therefore, I make a decree, that every people, nation, and language which speaks anything amiss against the God of Shadrach, Meshach, and Abednego shall be utterly destroyed, because there is no other God Who is able to deliver after this fashion."

Then he promoted the three brave young men to even higher posts of trust and responsibility in the province of Babylon.

This age-old story of faith and courage has inspired thousands of others ever since to stand for the right, no matter what it might cost. The great heroes and heroines of our faith have always been conscious that, in their fiery ordeal of suffering and martyrdom, there has been One beside them Whose form was "like the Son of God", as He was beside Shadrach, Meshach, and Abednego in their great trial by fire.

Daniel in the Lions' Den

Daniel does not appear to have been present when his three companions were thrown into the fiery furnace, because they refused to bow down before the golden image. No doubt there was good reason for his absence. He may have been ill, or away on some great matter of state. But Daniel's ordeal was to come.

The mighty Babylonian Empire had been overthrown by the Persians. The new King was Darius the Mede, who had brought with him the laws and customs of the Medes and Persians.

He divided his new kingdom into one hundred and twenty districts, each governed by a proconsul. These proconsuls, or governors, were responsible to three presidents, and of these three presidents Daniel was the first, "because an excellent spirit was in him".

This made the other high officials very jealous, and they wondered how they could catch him out in some matter in which they could report him to the King. But they could find no cause; for Daniel was faithful to his duty, and no error or fault could be found in him.

"Then said these men, We shall not find any occasion or fault against this Daniel, except we find it concerning the law of his God."

Now, these men knew that Daniel was in the habit of praying regularly three times a day to God, and this suggested to them a cunning plan in which to trap Daniel.

They went to the King and said to him, "King Darius, live

for ever. All the presidents of the kingdom, the governors, and the princes, the counsellors, and the captains, have consulted together to establish a royal statute, and to make a firm decree that whosoever shall ask a petition of any god or man for thirty days, save of thee, O King, he shall be cast into the den of lions. Now, O King, establish the decree, that it shall be unchangeable, according to the law of the Medes and Persians, which does not alter."

This is the old trick which has been used to flatter dictators even to this very day, and Darius was deceived by it, as they all are. He signed the decree without foreseeing the consequences.

When Daniel knew the decree had been signed, he went into his house, and opened the windows which faced in the direction of Jerusalem, and kneeled down three times a day, praying and giving thanks to God, just as he had always done.

This, of course, was just what his enemies had been waiting for. They hurried to the King, and said to him, "Did your majesty not sign a decree which forbade anyone asking a petition of any god or man within a period of thirty days, except from you, your majesty, on the penalty of being cast into the den of lions?"

The King replied that he certainly had done so, and that the decree stood firm, according to the law of the Medes and Persians that once a law was made it stood for ever.

"Well," they cried with triumphant delight, "that Daniel, who was brought from Judah as a prisoner-of-war, pays no attention to you or to your decree. He goes on praying to his own God, three times a day, just as he did before."

Then the King saw how he had been trapped, and called himself all kinds of fool for being so easily taken in. He tried very hard to save Daniel, but he was always countered by the reminder about the laws of the Medes and Persians which could not be altered once the King had signed them.

So the King at last gave in, and Daniel was seized and thrown into the den of lions. But before he was put into the den, the King said to Daniel, "Your God Whom you serve so faithfully will deliver you."

Then the door of the den was sealed with the seals of the King and of his counsellors, so that the King could not change his mind and try to rescue Daniel during the night.

The King could not sleep that night, and as soon as it was daylight he hurried to the den of lions, and called down to Daniel in a tearful voice, " O Daniel, servant of the living God, is your God Whom you serve so faithfully able to deliver you from the lions? "

In a voice that was firm and free from any note of fear, Daniel replied, " O King, live for ever. My God has sent His angel and has shut the mouths of the lions, and they have not hurt me, because I kept my trust before God. And I have done your cause no harm, O King."

The King was overjoyed, and commanded that Daniel should be lifted up out of the den of lions, and everybody could see that the hungry lions had not done him the least harm, because he had been trusting in God all the time.

Darius made another decree that in every part of his great empire men should show reverence for Daniel's God, " for He is the living God, and endures for ever, and His kingdom never shall be destroyed, and his dominion shall have no end. He delivers and rescues. He does signs and wonders in heaven and in earth. He has delivered Daniel from the power of the lions."

Because men like Daniel and his three companions have stood firm in the face of evil tyranny we enjoy the liberty we have to-day.

The Prophet Who Ran Away

The little book of Jonah, which has only four small chapters, opens with these simple words : " Now the word of the Lord came to Jonah, the son of Amittai, saying, Arise and go to Nineveh, that great city, and cry against it : for their wickedness is come up before me."

132

Nineveh was the capital city of the Assyrian empire which conquered Israel. It lay away to the far north-east. But Jonah, instead of taking the long camel route overland to the far east, went by sea to the far west in the opposite direction.

He went down to the port of Joppa and, finding there a ship going to Tarshish, paid the fare to take him there. Some people think that Tarshish was Tartessus, on the coast of Spain. Wherever it was, it was so far away for those days that the Jews regarded it as almost out of the world altogether —a place outside even of "the presence of God"! .

Now, why did Jonah want to get away from the presence of God, instead of obeying the word of God which was that he should go to Nineveh? Before we try to answer that, let us see what happened to Jonah after he went on board the ship bound for Tarshish.

Soon after they had sailed from Joppa, a great storm got up, and it looked as if the ship would be lost with all on board. The sailors did all they could to save the ship, and every man kept praying to his favourite god to save him.

Where do you think Jonah was all this time? He was down in the cabin sound asleep! "What are you sleeping there for," said the captain, as he tried to waken him. "Get up, and call on your God to save us."

But it made no difference, and, at last, the sailors decided to cast lots to find out who on board might be responsible for the trouble they were in. And the lot fell on Jonah!

The sailors said to Jonah, "Who are you? What are you doing here? What is your occupation? Where do you come from, and what is your nationality?"

"I am a Hebrew," replied Jonah, "and I worship Jehovah, the God of heaven, who made the sea and the dry land. I am on board fleeing from the presence of God."

"Why have you done this to us?" they cried. "What are we to do to you to make the sea calm?" For the seas were rising higher and higher over the ship.

"Take me up," said Jonah, "and throw me into the sea, and it will be calm for you. For I know it is because of me that the storm has overtaken you."

The sailors did not want to do such a thing, and they rowed hard to get the ship to shore, but at last they had to give it up. So they took Jonah and threw him into the sea, and there was a great calm.

The sailors prayed that God would not punish them for throwing Jonah into the sea, for they had done it only because they felt that somehow it was God's will it should be done.

It was, indeed, God's will, as Jonah himself realized. It was a foolish thing to think that he could go anywhere where God was not present. " Whither shall I go from Thy Spirit? " cried the Psalmist, " Or whither shall I flee from Thy presence? . . . If I take the wings of the morning and dwell in the uttermost parts of the sea : even there shall Thy hand lead me, and Thy right hand shall hold me."

In the depths of the sea, Jonah thought of the strange experience through which he was passing. " In the midst of my trouble, I cried unto the Lord, and He answered me. From the deepest depths I called to Him, and He heard me. When my soul fainted within me, I remembered the Lord : and my prayer reached up to His holy presence. I will sacrifice unto Thee with the voice of thanksgiving; what I have promised to do, that will I do. Salvation is of the Lord."

Then God commanded the great fish to put Jonah on the dry land, and spoke to Jonah the second time. " Go to Nineveh, that great city, and preach there the message I commanded you."

Jonah did not hesitate this time. He went to the great city of Nineveh, and for one whole day he proclaimed, " Yet forty days, and Nineveh shall be overthrown."

The effect of this message was electric. The people of Nineveh at once believed the word that had come from God through His prophet Jonah. The King immediately ordered that everyone in Nineveh from the greatest to the least should dress in sackcloth as a sign of great sorrow, and should taste neither food nor water as a sign of repentance. Even the animals were to fast as well as the rich and the poor.

The King, himself dressed in sackcloth, ordered that every-

Jonah is cast ashore by the whale.

one should turn from their evil ways, and that all should cry earnestly to God. "For who can tell," he said, "if God will not relent, and turn from his fierce anger, and not punish us as we deserve."

When God saw how the people of Nineveh had taken to heart Jonah's warning, and had given up their evil ways, and were truly sorry for what they had done, He did forgive them, and promised He would not punish them as He had purposed to do when He first sent Jonah to them.

Jonah's Object Lesson

Was Jonah pleased when by his preaching the people of Nineveh repented and were saved? He was not! He was very angry, and so God had to try by another way to teach the prophet the lesson he was so slow to learn.

Jonah had climbed a little hill just outside Nineveh, and

was sitting there waiting, and, no doubt, hoping for destruction to come upon the city.

The sun was very hot, as he sat there waiting, and there was no shade. So God prepared a gourd, a leafy kind of plant, to grow up over Jonah to give him shelter from the fierce heat. Jonah was very thankful for the shade.

Then just as suddenly the gourd withered up, and the sun beat down on the head of Jonah and he fainted. When he recovered, he was annoyed with the whole business, and very upset about the gourd.

Then God said to him, "Do you think you are right to be so troubled about the gourd in this manner?" "Why, of course, I am right to be troubled about the gourd," replied Jonah, "it meant so much to me."

"You think it right to be troubled about a plant which grew in a night, and withered in a night," God said to him, "and yet you do not think it is right for Me to be troubled about the great city of Nineveh, in which there are more than a hundred and twenty thousand little children, let alone grown-up people?"

You see, what Jonah was really angry about was that God should spare Nineveh at all. "O Lord," he had said to God, when God relented from being angry with the people of Nineveh, "was this not what I thought when I was still in my own country? I fled to Tarshish: for I knew that you are a gracious God, and merciful, slow to anger, and of great kindness, and always ready to relent. Therefore, now, O Lord, take my life, for it is better for me to die than to live."

Jonah was a very patriotic Israelite, and hated the Assyrians because of their cruelty to the Jewish people. He sincerely thought that the best thing that could happen for his people was the total destruction of the capital city of their greatest enemies.

He knew that if the people of Nineveh were warned of the danger they were in, they might repent and be saved. He did not want to warn them, and so he tried to "flee from the presence of the Lord".

The book of Jonah is a precious little book, because away

back in those far-off days when men were so cruel, it taught the love and mercy of God. Long before the New Testament times, when the Lord Jesus came to teach men to love their enemies, because all men are children of the same heavenly Father, this little book of only four chapters was teaching, not only the prophet Jonah but also all the Jews that every man, woman and child in the world is precious in the sight of God.

END OF
OLD TESTAMENT STORIES

The First Christmas

"The little Lord Jesus asleep on the hay."

Mary was a sweet and gentle girl who lived in Nazareth. She was engaged to be married to Joseph, the village carpenter. Joseph was a good, kind man, and, like Mary, he loved God and was ready to do whatever God might ask of him.

One day the angel Gabriel suddenly appeared to Mary and announced the wonderful news that the Son of God was coming into the world as a helpless little Baby, and that she was to be this Baby's mother.

In the same way an angel came to Joseph to tell him that he was to share the sacred trust of caring for the Holy Child.

"Joseph, son of David," said the angel, "fear not to take

Mary as your wife for the Baby that will be known as your son, will be none other than the Son of God. When the Holy Child is born, you shall call his name JESUS, for he shall save his people from their sins." So the Baby's name was ready for Him before He came—JESUS.

In those days, Palestine was part of the great Roman empire, and just about the time when Joseph and Mary set up their home in the carpenter's shop in Nazareth, the Roman emperor issued an order that everyone in his empire should pay a poll tax; that is, the payment of a fixed sum of money for every person.

The manner in which the tax was collected was for each person to go to the place to which he belonged. This meant that some people who had left their home-town or village would have to make the journey back to it no matter where they happened to be.

Now, because Joseph was of the house of David, he had to go to Bethlehem, the city of David, and Mary, his young wife, had to go with him.

Joseph would have to make many preparations for the journey, especially for the care and comfort of Mary. He would have to get a donkey for her to ride on, and perhaps another donkey to carry the things they would need while they were away.

Some people think that amongst other things Joseph, the carpenter, made a manger for the donkeys' hay, and, as he made it, designed it for another use as well. A manger can quite easily be used as a cradle.

When they got to Bethlehem, they found the place crowded with people who had come to pay their taxes. There was no room for them to stay anywhere, not even in the one poor inn of which the town boasted.

Poor Joseph! how anxious he must have been, as he searched for a room for his sweet, little wife. Perhaps the innkeeper was sorry for them, and suggested that they might care to spend the night in a corner of the stable of the inn. It would at least be warm, for it was a bitterly cold night outside.

During that night, Mary's Baby was born. According to eastern custom, she wrapped Him in swaddling clothes, which means she swathed Him in linen clothes or bandages, so that the Baby was protected from the cold. Then, because there was no proper cradle, like the one that would certainly be waiting for Him at home in Nazareth, Mary laid the Baby Jesus in a manger.

"While Shepherds Watched"

The stars in the East seem to shine more brightly than they do for us in the West. Against the deep blue velvet of the night, they sparkle in the sky like diamonds. On this clear, frosty night the Bethlehem shepherds lay all around their camp fire, each man muffled in his long cloak right up to his eyes because of the cold.

As they lay gazing up to the stars, they spoke in quiet whispers to one another, listening all the while for any movement amongst the sheep that might tell that some wild animal was prowling about.

Suddenly, they saw a light in the sky brighter than any star. It grew larger and larger, came nearer and nearer, until a heavenly light shone all around them. Then they saw an angel standing in the centre of this unearthly brightness, and they fell on their faces, afraid.

"Don't be afraid," said the angel, "for it is good news I bring to you: glad tidings of great joy for all the people of the world. To-day in the city of David, the Saviour of the world has been born. This is how you will know Him: you will find a Baby wrapped in swaddling clothes, lying in a manger."

As the angel spoke, a great company of other angels joined him, and the heavenly choir sang the first Christmas carol ever heard on earth:

140

An angel brings the good news to the shepherds.

Glory to God in highest heaven,
And on earth peace to men of good will.

Then the heavenly light faded away, and only the stars in the dark sky were left shining.

The shepherds gazed at one another in wonder. "Let us go now to Bethlehem," they said, "and see this wonderful thing which the Lord has told us about," and they hurried up the hill-path to the town, eager to find the Baby.

The angel had given them a clue—the *Baby wrapped in swaddling clothes, lying in a manger*. The stable of the inn would be a likely place to begin with, and there sure enough they found Him. There was the Baby in a manger; near by, the sweet little mother, and, standing behind, concerned and caring for them both, was good Joseph.

The shepherds were greatly excited, and they tried to tell everybody in the inn and round about that this was no ordinary Baby, for angels from heaven had told them wonderful things about Him, when they were in the fields. But it did not make sense to the others. Who could believe the story of a Saviour born in a stable?

Mary listened to the shepherds' story of the angel and the heavenly choir with their good news of glad tidings, and she pondered all these things in her heart.

As for the shepherds, they had no doubt at all about what they had seen and heard, and they returned to their flocks glorifying and praising God.

Do you not think that it was a very lovely thing that it should have been shepherds who were the first to worship Jesus? When, thirty years later, Jesus began to teach the people, He often talked about sheep and shepherds. Speaking of Himself, He said, " I am the Good Shepherd : the good shepherd gives his life for the sheep."

As we shall see later on, this was what Jesus came to do—to give His life for those who, like sheep, have gone astray from God.

The Guiding Star

One morning a strange little procession rode into Jerusalem. There was nothing very surprising about that, for the people of Jerusalem were accustomed to seeing all kinds of strange visitors. What was surprising about this particular group was the kind of question they were asking: "Where is He that is born King of the Jews? for we have seen His star in the east, and are come to worship Him."

The Bible describes these strangers as "wise men from the east". An old story, not in the Bible, tells us that there were three of them, because of the three gifts which they had brought with them, and that their names were—Melchior, Caspar, and Balthasar. But the only thing we really know about them is that they studied the stars. They had seen a new and specially bright star in the sky, and from their knowledge of the stars believed it to mean that a new King of the Jews had been born in Palestine.

Another thing we may safely say about them is that they were not only wise but also religious, for they realized that the new King was, in some special sense, sent by God, and they felt they must undertake the long and difficult journey in order to worship Him.

Now, at that time, the King of Judah was a particularly horrid person called Herod. He was King only so long as he did what the Romans told him to do. Provided he did that, he could do pretty well what else he liked, and Herod did very much as he liked.

Herod had his spies everywhere, and what the wise men were asking soon got to his ears. "Where is He that is born King of the Jews?" He was full of suspicion, always smelling out plots, and this looked like some kind of plot. "He was troubled and all Jerusalem with him."

We know that the Jewish people were eagerly expecting the coming of One Who would deliver them from their enemies. And that, for the time being, meant the hated Romans. Herod knew that anyone who wished to get rid of the Romans would want to get rid of him too. So he summoned all the chief priests and other religious leaders of the people to his palace, and demanded that they should tell him where the promised King was to be born.

" In Bethlehem of Judaea," they replied, " for this is how it was written by the prophet; ' And you, Bethlehem, in the land of Juda, are not the least among the princes of Juda, for out of you will come a Governor, that will rule my people Israel '."

So much for the place, but what about the time? Herod had a private talk with the wise men to find out when it was exactly that they saw the star they had spoken of. When he found out that the new King of Judah the wise men were seeking for could only be a baby, he directed them to Bethlehem and said, "Go search diligently for the young Child; and when you have found Him, let me know, that I may follow after you and worship also."

But the wise men had no need to search diligently, for when they left the palace, there was the star to guide them still. They followed it until it stopped over the place where the Holy Child lay.

We do not know if the Holy Family was still in the stable. Probably not, for the Bible speaks of the wise men going into a house : " And when they were come into the house, they saw the young Child with Mary His mother, and fell down, and worshipped Him : and when they opened their treasures, they presented to Him gifts of gold, frankincense, and myrrh." These were royal gifts, such as they would have brought to give to a King.

The wise men did not return to tell Herod they had found the King they had been searching for. God warned them in a dream of Herod's wicked plans, and they returned to their own country by another way.

Christmas time, when we remember the coming of Jesus as a Baby to Bethlehem, is the season of gifts. It is pleasant to think of this first Christmas, and good to remember those wise men from the East who were the first to begin the custom of giving presents at Christmastide.

The Flight into Egypt

When Herod realized that the wise men had not been deceived by him, but had returned to their own country without telling him where the Holy Child was, he fell into a terrible rage, and in his anger and spiteful hate issued an order which has shocked the world ever since.

He sent his soldiers to Bethlehem and commanded that every child under two years of age, in Bethlehem and round about, should be put to death. Herod calculated the period from the time the wise men had first seen the star in the east.

This "massacre of the innocents", as it has been called, reminded Matthew of the prophecy of Jeremiah, in the Old Testament; "In Rama was heard the sound of lamentation, and weeping, and great mourning. Rachel weeping for her children, and refusing to be comforted, because they are gone."

But Herod's wicked plan failed of its purpose, for an angel had warned Joseph in a dream, "Rise up quickly, and take the young Child and His mother, and escape into Egypt, and stay there until I tell you to return, for Herod will seek for the young Child and try to destroy Him."

That same night, the Holy Family took the long road to Egypt and to safety. The gold which the wise men had given to the young Child would now be useful, for Joseph would require money for the journey and for their stay in Egypt.

How long they remained in Egypt we are not told, but it could not have been for very long, for Jesus was still very young when the angel came to Joseph again in a dream, and said, "Arise, and take the young Child and His mother, and return to the land of Israel, for they are dead who sought the young Child's life."

Joseph seems to have thought at first of going back to Bethlehem, but when he heard that Archelaus, a son of Herod, and almost as bad a man as his father, was now King of Judah, he hesitated. But again the angel directed him, and Joseph took Mary and Jesus to Galilee.

The district of Galilee was actually ruled over by another son of Herod whose name was Herod Antipas. He was by no means a good man, but he was not nearly so bad as his father had been or his brother was. So Joseph felt they would be safe in Galilee.

And to what better place in Galilee could they go than to Nazareth, their old home town, where they were well known, and where they had many friends? There, too, Joseph could take up again his work as a carpenter.

Nazareth was about three days' journey on foot north from Jerusalem, and built on one of the foot-hills of Lebanon. Above it was a higher hill, from which could be seen Mount Carmel, with its snow-covered summit, and the Mediterranean Sea away in the distance. Below it was a valley which, in their seasons, was covered with many lovely wild-flowers and all kinds of fruit.

While it was a quiet, secluded village, not far away ran the main road along which continually passed the pilgrims to Jerusalem, the marching cohorts of Rome, and the camel-trains of merchants from Egypt, Europe, and Asia.

To this very day, the main water supply in the town is called the Virgin's Well, where Mary must often have drawn the water for the household.

Jesus lived in Nazareth until He was thirty, so that although He was born in Bethlehem, He came to be known as Jesus of Nazareth.

The Boyhood of Jesus

The Bible tells us very little about the boyhood of Jesus. Practically all we do know is told in the Gospel written by Luke, "the beloved physician". And Luke gives us really only one incident of Jesus as a boy. But what a wonderful story it is!

146

When a Jewish boy became twelve or thirteen, he was expected to attend the Temple in Jerusalem, and become "a son of the commandment". From that time, he was regarded as a full member of the Jewish Church, sharing in all its duties and privileges. So, when Jesus was twelve, His parents took Him to Jerusalem.

It was at the time of the great Feast of the Passover when

Jesus astonishes the teachers in the Temple.

thousands of pilgrims went up to Jerusalem from all over Palestine and, indeed, from many different parts of the world as well.

At Passover time, people of the same town or village would form themselves into parties for safety and companionship. So Joseph and Mary joined the party going from Nazareth. It must have been a happy party. There would be much to see on the road, and much to talk about. At night, it would be thrilling to sleep under the stars.

How thrilled Jesus must have felt to catch His first glimpse

147

of Jerusalem, with the morning sun reflected from the spires of gold!

As He mingled with the crowds of pilgrims thronging the Temple, passing along its terraces and colonnades of white marble and gleaming gold, all leading to the Sanctuary with its Holy of Holies, his mind must have turned to His Father in Heaven Whose will on earth He had come to do.

At the end of the Passover, Joseph and Mary joined the Nazareth party for the homeward journey. At the end of the first day, when they were making camp for the night, they looked for Jesus, but could not find Him. They had been under the impression all that day that Jesus had been travelling along with some of His young friends, but when they made enquiries among their relatives and acquaintances, they found that these folk had not seen the Boy all day.

Mary and Joseph hurried back to Jerusalem, and called at the various places where they had stayed or had visited during the Passover. But Jesus was nowhere to be found.

At last, they thought of the Temple and made their way there. As they were going along one of the pillared terraces, they came across a group of religious teachers, and there in the midst of them was Jesus!

As they drew near to the group, they could see that everyone was amazed at the kind of questions Jesus was asking the teachers, and the kind of answers He was returning to their questions. For a boy of twelve, his knowledge and understanding of the Old Testament greatly astonished them all.

Mary went forward to Jesus, and said, "My Son, why have you frightened us like this? Your father and I have been anxiously searching for you."

"Why did you search for Me?" Jesus replied. "Did you not know I had to be about My Father's business?"

They did not understand Him then, but, as Luke tells us, "His mother kept all these sayings in her heart."

Luke also goes on to say that Jesus "went down with them, and came to Nazareth, and was obedient to them. . . . And Jesus increased in wisdom and stature, and in favour with God and man."

The Home in Nazareth

Nazareth has, of course, changed in many ways in 2,000 years, but not so much as to make it too difficult for us to imagine what it looked like when Jesus was a boy. For when He lived in Nazareth, Jesus lived, played, and worked just like the other boys round about Him.

Jesus probably lived in a little stone house with only one room. It would have a flat roof reached by an outside stairway of stone steps. In the hot summer weather, the family slept on the roof. It must have been great fun lying in bed looking up to the bright stars twinkling in the night sky.

The little room, with its hard clay floor, would have hardly any furniture. There would be a few rush mats on the floor perhaps, and a large wooden chest in which to keep the best clothes, and the few family treasures. Some jars would be standing against the wall in which to store the water, wine, olive oil, and corn.

At meal times, the family would sit, cross-legged, tailor-fashion, round a low table, or large brass tray. One large dish would be placed on the table, containing a rich stew of rice, meat, or fish, and vegetables. Each member of the family would have one or two little loaves of toasted wheatmeal. This they would break into small pieces and dip them, in turn, into the common dish, using the bread like little scoops or spoons.

Going to bed at night was a simple affair in that little house. Bed-mats were unrolled and spread on the floor, and the whole family would sleep in their day clothes, with perhaps an extra cloak thrown over them.

Outside the house would be the little hand-mill, with its upper- and nether-stones for grinding the corn. Mary and her next-door neighbour would grind the corn, for it required two women to do it, the flour escaping through a little hole in the lower stone. Outside, too, would be the oven for baking the flat, round loaves. Twigs and dried grass were used to heat the oven before the dough was put into it.

In front of the house, or leaning up against the side of it, would be the carpenter's shop with its heap of shavings and nice smell of new wood.

After helping Mary to roll up the bed-mats, and get the oven going for the simple morning meal, Jesus would go off to school. The little village school was really the synagogue,

Jesus at work in his father's workshop.

and the local rabbi, or minister, the teacher. There Jesus and the other boys would learn to read or write. Girls were not sent to school.

There would be no seats or desks in the school Jesus attended. The pupils just sat on the floor around the teacher, who sat on a little platform not much higher than the floor.

There would be no books, for there was no printing in those days, but a few scrolls on which would be written parts of the Old Testament. Learning was mostly by reciting singly or all together in a kind of chant. The boys were well drilled in the Jewish law and prophets.

In the afternoons, Jesus would help Joseph in the carpenter's shop. There He would learn how to use the adze, which is a kind of hammer, chisel, and plane all in one. He would learn how to use the saw, pushing it away from him, and not pulling it to him, as our joiners do.

He would make holes with the whirling drill, and wooden pins, or nails, to hammer into them with a mallet. He would learn how to sharpen and handle the carving and smoothing tools for the finer work, and how to choose and fell the right kind of trees for the different kinds of jobs.

Joseph would make all kinds of things in his little workshop —houses and furniture, barns and farming implements. Jesus, for example, knew how to make yokes so smooth and so well-balanced that they would not chafe or hurt the neck of the oxen.

In the evening, before it got quickly dark, as it does in the East, Jesus would play games in the streets with His companions. They would play all kinds of games, some of them not unlike the games you play with your friends. Jesus actually mentions two of the games in one of His parables. He speaks of the children playing in the market place at weddings and funerals.

As Jesus grew too old for games, He loved to take long walks into the country. In His parables we have many memories of those rambles, for Jesus speaks of the birds, and the flowers, of the shepherds and their sheep, and of the farmers working in their fields—ploughing and then sowing, reaping and then threshing the corn.

We know that Jesus went to the synagogue every Sabbath day to worship God. There He listened to the Scriptures being read and explained, and joined in the prayers and the psalms.

Joseph seems to have died while Jesus was still a young man, and so Jesus would become the breadwinner for the family. It was then He learned how hard life was for the ordinary peasant in Palestine. He knew how very careful

Mary had to be with the food, and the clothes, and the money that was so hardly earned.

In later years, His parables were to tell of the grinding of the corn, of the leaven in the meal, of the patching of old garments, and the anxious searching for the lost coin so badly needed to pay the family debts or, perhaps, the taxes.

Only one who lived through it all could have known so well the life of the hard-working peasant in Palestine, and for thirty years Jesus lived the life of an ordinary peasant in a very ordinary little village where He was known as The Carpenter.

John the Baptist

News travels quickly in the little land of Palestine, and one day exciting news was brought to Nazareth—a new prophet had appeared in the land, and was engaging in a religious crusade on the banks of the river Jordan away down in Judah, not far from Jerusalem itself.

There had been no prophet in Israel, like Elijah or Elisha, for hundreds of years, and the exciting news of this strange prophet spread from village to village. Great crowds flocked to hear him.

He had a very strange appearance, this prophet. He actually reminded men of Elijah, so stern and rugged did he look. He was dressed in a long cloak woven of camels' hair, and a leather belt tight round his waist.

His food was the plain food the very poor people ate—locusts, which are insects like huge grasshoppers, and honey which the wild bees stored up in the cracks of the desert rocks. For this fiery preacher lived all by himself in the desert.

His message was as simple and stern as he was himself. He called the people to "flee from the wrath to come"; to repent from their sins, and to do good deeds as proof of changed lives.

He warned the people that they were on the eve of great happenings. They were not to imagine that because they were Jews, they were better than other people. In the new Kingdom that was about to come, all that mattered would be not a man's nationality, but a man's nature.

Hundreds were convinced of the truth of his message, and, as a sign that they were sorry for their sins and wished to live new lives, were baptised by John in the river Jordan. Because of this, he was known as John the Baptist.

The news about this prophet was specially exciting for Mary's household in Nazareth, for this John was none other than the son of her cousin Elisabeth.

Luke tells us that when John was born, his father Zacharias said of him, "You, child, will be called the prophet of the Highest: for you will go before the face of the Lord, to prepare His ways: to give knowledge of salvation to His people, by the forgiveness of their sins, through the tender mercy of our God: whereby the Dayspring from on high has come to us: to give light to those who sit in darkness, and in the shadow of death, to guide our feet into the way of peace."

Like Jesus, John the Baptist seems to have spent his early life hidden away in some quiet place, and now, at the age of thirty, he suddenly bursts into public view, "a burning and a shining light", to prepare the way of the Lord.

It seems to have been the signal for which Jesus was waiting. Quietly He left Nazareth, and made His way to the banks of the Jordan.

As John saw Him coming, he pointed to Jesus, and cried, "Behold, the Lamb of God who beareth away the sin of the world."

To John's amazement, Jesus came down into the water like the others to be baptised. "Why," he asked himself, "should the Son of God come to me to be baptised? He has no sin that He needs to repent."

At first, he declined to do what Jesus asked. "I have need to be baptised of you," he said, "and yet you come to me!"

But Jesus quietly said to John, "You must baptise me, for only in this way can we do the righteous will of God."

John then baptised Jesus, and, as they were coming up out of the water, the heavens seemed to open and John saw what he thought to be a beautiful white dove, resting upon the shoulder of Jesus. And he heard a Voice from heaven saying, "This is my well-loved Son, in whom I am well pleased."

This wonderful scene on the banks of the river Jordan marks the beginning of the ministry of Jesus. For three brief years, He was to walk the paths and lanes of Palestine "preaching the gospel of the kingdom of God", healing the sick, and even raising the dead.

The Programme of Jesus

Jesus first of all began to teach the people in His own country of Galilee. After a little while He returned to His own town of Nazareth, and on the Sabbath day He went, as was His practice, to the synagogue.

In the synagogue, it was the custom to ask one of the men, especially if he were a stranger or a returning visitor, to read a passage from the Scriptures and then to say what he thought the passage meant.

On this particular Sabbath day, Jesus was asked to read. When the scroll was handed to Him, Jesus read a passage from the prophet Isaiah:

"The Spirit of the Lord is come upon me, because he hath anointed me to preach the gospel to the poor: he has sent me to heal the broken-hearted, to preach deliverance to the captives, and recovering of sight to the blind, to set at liberty them that are bruised, to preach the year of grace of the Lord."

Jesus then rolled up the scroll, handed it back to the
154

minister, and sat down. But everybody looked intently at Him, waiting for His explanation of the passage He had chosen.

So Jesus began again, and said, "This day is the scripture fulfilled in your ears." And He went on to explain to them that this passage was the programme He had come to carry out : that He had indeed come to set up God's Kingdom on earth—the Kingdom in which there would be no harmful thing, but only love, joy, and peace.

Now, Jesus knew He could not do this great work all by Himself, but that He would require others to help Him. One day, as He was walking along the shore of the lake of Galilee, He saw two fishermen together casting a net into the sea, and He said to them, "Follow Me, and I will make you fishers of men." The two men immediately laid down their net and followed Jesus. They were two brothers, Peter and Andrew.

Going farther along the shore, they saw two other fishermen. They were working beside a boat, mending their nets, along with some others. Jesus said to them, "Follow Me," and they left the boat and followed Him. They, too, were brothers, James and John. They left the boat in the charge of their father Zebedee, with a small crew of hired men to help him.

On another occasion, Jesus was walking through one of the little ports on the lake of Galilee, and He saw a Customs Officer sitting at his desk. Jesus said to him, "Follow Me," and the man immediately got up and followed Him. This man's name was Matthew.

Andrew and Peter belonged to the city of Bethsaida. There they found their friend Philip, and introduced him to their new Master. Jesus said to Philip, "Follow Me."

Philip not only followed Jesus himself, but he also brought along a friend. The name of this friend was Nathanael. "We have found Him," Philip cried joyfully to Nathanael, "of whom Moses in the law, and the prophets did write— Jesus of Nazareth, the son of Joseph."

Nathanael was doubtful at first. "Can any good thing come out of Nazareth?" he said to Philip. He meant that

Nazareth was so small and insignificant that it could not possibly produce any great person.

Philip simply replied, "Come and see." Nathanael did come, and what he saw and heard made him certain Philip was right. "Teacher," he said to Jesus, "You are the Son of God; You are the King of Israel."

Now, that made seven altogether, and so the little band grew until there was quite a company of men, and women, too, who believed that Jesus had been sent by God.

Jesus calls Matthew to follow him.

When Jesus said "Follow Me", He meant it in two ways. First, He meant, "Come with Me; listen to My teaching; see the way in which I live, and the things that I do."

Secondly, He meant, "Follow My way in your own lives. Do the things I tell you to do in all your conduct day by day." They were to be His disciples; that is to say, they were to learn of Him like scholars in the school of Jesus.

In Palestine it was no strange thing to see a teacher going about with his disciples. Some of the disciples of Jesus stayed with Him all the time, some would go to their homes and come back again for a while.

Luke tells us that one night Jesus went on to a mountain-side alone, and spent the whole night in prayer to God. And then he tells us why Jesus did this. The next day, Jesus called His disciples to Him, and from amongst them He chose twelve to be Apostles.

" Apostle " means one who is specially chosen for a particular mission, and Jesus wished to have those twelve men to be with Him all the time. He wanted them to hear all He said so that they might carry on His work after He had gone.

And so those twelve had the glorious privilege that no other group of men has ever had in the whole of history—of walking with Jesus through the Holy Land, listening to all the wonderful things Jesus had to tell them, and seeing all the amazing miracles which He did. Above all, they lived day by day with Him Who was without fault of any kind, and Who was so good and kind in all He did.

The Apostles were a very mixed team indeed, all different from one another, and sometimes showing it by quarrelling amongst themselves. One was to betray Him to His enemies, and all of them were to desert Him in the hour of His greatest need, but Jesus loved them all, and was so patient with them.

And they learned to love Him so much in return that nearly all of them were to die for His sake in the years that lay ahead. Through their work and sacrifice the gospel He came to proclaim was carried to the whole world.

~~~~~~~~~~~~~~~~~~~~~~~~~~~~~~~~~~~~~~~

The Box of Precious Ointment

Jesus was once invited to dinner by a religious leader of the Jews called Simon. His invitation seems to have been prompted by curiosity rather than genuine love for our Lord, for he omitted three little courtesies usually shown to an invited guest. He did not order his servants to wash the feet of Jesus, or to anoint His head with oil. And when Jesus first arrived, he did not welcome Him with the customary kiss on the cheek.

While Jesus was sitting, or reclining, at the table, a woman came into the room who was known in all the town as a bad woman. In her hand she carried a lovely little box made of alabaster—a kind of thin marble beautifully carved. She went up to where Jesus was and stood behind His couch, tears flowing down her cheeks.

Kneeling down, she kissed the feet of Jesus. Her tears fell on His feet and she wiped them away with her lovely, long hair. Then, opening the little alabaster box, she anointed His feet with the precious, sweet-smelling ointment.

Now, Simon saw all this, and he said to himself, "If this man were the prophet he says he is, he would have known the kind of woman she is, and would have nothing to do with her."

Jesus knew what Simon was thinking, and He said to him, "Simon, I have something to say to you."

Simon replied, "Master, say on."

Then Jesus told Simon one of the lovely little stories He often told to carry home a lesson. A certain man was owed money by two other men. One owed five hundred pence; and the other, fifty pence. When he found they were unable to pay, he fully forgave them both.

"Tell Me," Jesus said to Simon, "which of the two would love him better."

"I suppose the one to whom he forgave most," replied Simon.

"Quite right," said Jesus, and then went on to teach Simon a lesson he would never forget.

"Do you see this woman, Simon," He said. "When I came into your house, you gave Me no water for My feet; but she has washed My feet with her tears, and wiped them with the hairs of her head. You gave Me no kiss; she has never ceased to kiss My feet since I came in. You did not anoint My head with oil; she has anointed My feet with this precious ointment. She has loved much, for her many sins are all forgiven. Those to whom little is forgiven, they love little."

Then Jesus turned to the poor woman, and assured her again that her sins were fully forgiven. Probably the woman had heard Jesus teaching the people in the open air the love of God and His readiness to forgive all who are really sorry for their sins, and this was the way she chose to show her gratitude.

Simon could only see the bad that was in the woman, and,

The woman pours the precious ointment on Jesus's feet,

for all he cared, she could go on from bad to worse. But Jesus saw the good woman she could become when she learned what true love really was, and He won her devotion because He was so good and kind to her. In this way, Jesus gathered many others around Him who were not afraid or ashamed to be known as His disciples.

Some of those who saw her breaking the alabaster box of the precious ointment over the feet of Jesus whispered to one another, "What a dreadful waste! Why couldn't that have been sold and the money given to the poor?"

159

Jesus heard them, and said to them, "Let her alone. Why do you discourage her like that? She wanted to show her grateful love for Me.

"You have the poor with you at any time, if you really want to help them; but Me you will not always have with you.

"This woman has done the only thing she could. She knows that My enemies will put Me to death, and she is showing Me her love while she may.

"I tell you this, wherever the gospel will be preached throughout the whole world, this thing she has done will be remembered as a memorial to her."

For two thousand years millions and millions of people have heard about this woman and her box of precious ointment, and have been inspired by her example to give fragrant service to God by helping their fellow men and women. And all over the world to-day they are still hearing about it.

The Young Man Who Said No

Once when Jesus was teaching the people, some mothers brought their children to Him so that He might bless them. The disciples told the mothers not to trouble the Master with so trifling a request, but to go away.

But Jesus called the mothers to Him, saying, "Let the little children come to Me, and forbid them not: for of such is the kingdom of God."

After Jesus had said good-bye to the children and was moving away, a young man came running after Him. We do not know his name, but we know he was a rich young man and held a position of importance and influence.

"Good Master," he said to Jesus, "what must I do to inherit the kingdom of God?"

Jesus, glancing keenly at him, said, "You know the commandments, do you not?"

160

"Yes," said the young man, "and I have obeyed them all, but I feel I still lack something in my life."

Jesus looked at the young man and loved him. "You lack one thing," He told him. "Sell all you have, and give it to the poor, and then come and follow Me."

When the young man heard this, he turned away, for he was very rich. He was not willing to give up his riches even for the kingdom of God. So he said no to the way of Jesus.

When Jesus saw how very sad the young man was, He said, "How hard it is for those who have riches to enter into the kingdom of God! It would be easier for a camel to go through the eye of a needle than for a rich man to enter into the kingdom of God."

What Jesus meant was that when a man gets to love his riches more than he loves God, it is almost impossible for him to become a true disciple. Jesus did not mean that only poor people could follow Him. Even poor people say no to Jesus when they would rather go their own way than follow His.

~~~~~~

Martha and Mary

Although Jesus had no home of His own, there were several homes in Palestine where He was always sure of a welcome. One was the house of two sisters called Martha and Mary.

Martha and Mary, and their brother Lazarus, too, were always delighted when Jesus paid them a visit. Each had his or her own way of showing it.

Martha was a very clever housewife, and whenever Jesus came to their home she bustled about, getting things ready. But Mary would sit at Jesus' feet and listen to His teaching.

One day, Martha got a little impatient at this, and she said, "Lord, do you not notice that my sister has left me to do all the serving? Tell her to come and help me."

Jesus looked up at Martha with a smile, and said very gently, " Martha, Martha, you are careful and worried about many things; but one thing is needful : and Mary has chosen that good part, and she will not be taken from it."

This little glimpse into a lovely house, where Jesus seemed to be so very much at home, has led to a great deal of discussion.

Many people sympathize with Martha, and feel that Jesus

Jesus with Mary and Martha.

was a little hard on her. These people feel that it was not very fair of Mary to sit still and let her sister do all the work. They point out that somebody has got to do the work, and we cannot all sit down like Mary, just listening and doing nothing.

Now, we have no reason to think that Mary was not just as good a housewife as Martha was. But Mary seems to have realized that she could not do two things at once—she could

162

not bustle about and listen to Jesus too. So she chose "that good part" which came her way all too seldom.

Jesus was no doubt very grateful for all Martha's kindly thought, but He would have preferred her to sit down as well, and listen to what He had to say to them both.

Jesus once told His disciples that He had come not to be served but to serve others. He was far more anxious to serve Martha than to be served by her, for Martha had far greater need to take what He had to give her.

Most people are like Martha. They are always eager to be *doing* something. They would far rather work a whole day for Jesus than spend a few minutes quietly listening to Him. But if they would only learn to spend a few minutes now and then each day praying to Jesus, and listening to what He has to say to them in His Word, they would be all the better able to do service for Him.

Building on the Rock

There was once a man who decided to build himself a house right down as near to the sea as he could get. Perhaps he thought it would be grand to run right out of the house, splash into the water! It was a lovely house. The man had spared no expense, and he was very proud and pleased with himself when he saw people passing along the shore admiring his summer palace.

He was annoyed when one day he discovered another house being built not far from his. It was on higher ground and farther back from the shore. He went over to see what was happening, and he was greatly amused when he saw the builders cutting deep down into the rock.

"What are they doing that for?" he asked his new neighbour.

"For the foundation," was the reply.

"Why go to all that trouble and expense?" he said. "I put my money mostly into the house itself," he continued, "and look at the fine result I have managed to get."

"Yes," replied his neighbour, "it's a grand house to be sure. All the same, I think I'll make sure of the foundation first."

When the second house was finished, it was smaller and plainer, and more homely looking than the first, as if the owner meant to live in it for ever.

"Silly fellow!" said the firstcomer to himself. "And he could have had much more comfort, had he followed my advice."

One dark night, a terrible storm sprang up. Down lashed the rain in swirling torrents. Crash came wave after wave on both houses. Blow after blow pounded on the walls, as the wind blew a hurricane.

With the coming of dawn, the storm had spent itself, and the man who had built his house on the rock looked out from his window. What a sad scene met his eyes! The house built on the sand below had been swept into the sea and not a trace remained.

"Oh!" he said sadly to his wife and children, "that must have been the terrible crash we heard above the storm last night. What a pity our poor neighbour built his house on the sand!"

Jesus once told a story like that. He had been teaching His disciples those wonderful lessons contained in what is known as the Sermon on the Mount. When He finished, He said, "Any one who hears these sayings of Mine and obeys them will be like a wise man who built his house on a rock. And everyone who hears these sayings of Mine and does not obey them will be like a man who built his house on the sand."

We are all builders, although not perhaps of houses made of stone. We are building up our characters by which other people know us. The materials we use are our thoughts, and words and deeds.

Some people are called "shifty" characters. They are weak

and cannot be depended upon. They are like the man who built his house on the sand.

Christian character is very different. It is a life that comes from obeying Jesus, trying to please Him in all we think and say and do. That is like building firmly on the rock. When trials and temptations come, as come they will, we shall stand strong and erect.

~~~~~~~~~~~~~~~~~~~~~~~~~~~~~~~~

The Story of the Good Samaritan

A crowd of people had gathered round the new Teacher and was plying Him with questions. Amongst the crowd was a lawyer who knew all about the Jewish law. Turning to one of his friends, he said, "Just listen to this. I'll trip Him up with a question or two."

"Master," he said to Jesus, "what must I do to gain eternal life?"

Jesus replied, "What does the law say about that? How do you understand it?"

The man replied, "The sum total of the law is, You will love the Lord your God with all your heart, and with all your soul, and with all your strength, and with all your mind; and love your neighbour as yourself."

"That is a good answer," said Jesus. "Now, go and do all that, and you will have eternal life."

The lawyer realized that Jesus had been too clever for him, and knew the crowd round about were smiling at him. So, to cover it up, he asked another difficult question. "And who is my neighbour?"

Instead of giving a direct reply to this question, Jesus told the story of the Good Samaritan.

A certain man went down from Jerusalem to Jericho. On a lonely part of the road, a band of robbers seized this man, beat him mercilessly, stripped him of everything, even his clothes, and left him lying on the road, naked and half-dead.

As the man lay there, a priest, returning home from the Temple in Jerusalem, came along, and, when he saw the poor man, crossed over to the other side of the road, and passed on.

Then there came a Levite, a priest of higher rank than the other. When he saw the man, he stopped and looked at him, and then hurried away. Probably they were afraid the robbers would attack them too.

Then there came along the road a traveller from Samaria. When he saw the dying man lying on the road, he was full of pity for him. He knelt down beside him, cleaned the man's wounds with wine, put soothing oil into the wounds and bandaged him up.

He then lifted the man up on to his horse, and took him to a nearby inn. There he did what he could to get the poor man well. But he had to go on his journey again, and he said to the keeper of the inn, "Here is some money, take care of him, and if this money is not enough, I will pay you more when I come this way again."

"Now," Jesus asked the lawyer, "which of these three—the priest, the Levite, or the Samaritan—was neighbour to him that fell among the thieves?"

"He that had pity on him and helped him," replied the lawyer.

In this way Jesus showed the clever lawyer that it was not enough to know what the law says, but what the law means. For the point of the story of the Good Samaritan is this, the Jews hated the Samaritans and would have nothing to do with them. But it was a Samaritan who helped a Jew in trouble when the priest and Levite, very religious Jews, passed by on the other side.

A Jew thought he was keeping the law when he helped a fellow-Jew, but to help a foreigner, let alone a Samaritan, was something new!

There are some stories which we call "revolutionary"; that is, they completely change the way in which people are in the habit of thinking and behaving. The story of the Good

The Levite passes by the injured man.

Samaritan is one of the most " revolutionary" stories ever told. For the first time, men were taught that they were to regard as their neighbour anybody, friend or foreigner, who was in need of help.

The Shepherd and the Sheep

In Eastern countries, the shepherd does not drive his flock before him, as our shepherds do. He goes before his sheep and they follow him.

The Eastern shepherd knows each one of his sheep, sometimes even by name. They know his voice and his peculiar whistle. If two or more flocks get mixed up—at the watering place, for example—the shepherd has only to make his own special sound or whistle and the sheep sort themselves out. If a stranger were to call to them, they would pay no

167

attention to him, "for they know not the voice of strangers".

During the day, the shepherd leads his flock to where they may find green pastures, and pools of clean, cool water. Sometimes there are enemies lurking about in the form of poisonous snakes or wild beasts. The shepherd kills the snakes, or stops up their holes, and drives the wild beasts away. Often he has to lead the sheep through dangerous-looking valleys where the sheep are apt to slip down. The shepherd keeps them safe with his rod and staff.

The good shepherd searches for his lost sheep.

Towards evening, the shepherd leads the flock home. Sometimes he may have to carry a lame sheep across his shoulder, or a young lamb in his arms. When night comes, he gathers his sheep into a fold, which may be a large cave, or a small stone enclosure. He counts the sheep as they go into the fold to see if any are missing. As he counts them, he looks them over very thoroughly to see if any are hurt in any way, and rubs oil over the sore places.

When all the sheep are folded, the shepherd lies down at the entrance so that no sheep can get out, and no wild animal can get in without his knowing it. *He* is the door.

So you see how in a land like Palestine there is a closer bond between the shepherd and the sheep than there is in this country. The care of the shepherd for his sheep reminded some of the poets and prophets of Israel of God's care for His people. The twenty-third psalm, for example, tells of God's shepherd-care.

The Lord is my shepherd: I shall not want.
He maketh me to lie down in green pastures; he leadeth me
* beside the still waters.*
He restoreth my soul; he leadeth me in the paths of
* righteousness for his name's sake.*
Yea, though I walk through the valley of the shadow of
* death, I will fear no evil; for thou art with me; thy rod*
* and thy staff they comfort me.*
Thou preparest a table before me in the presence of mine
* enemies; thou anointest my head with oil; my cup run-*
* neth over.*
Surely goodness and mercy shall follow me all the days of
* my life: and I will dwell in the house of the Lord for ever.*

Now, God's love for us is seen best of all in His Son, our Saviour, and Jesus spoke of Himself as the Good Shepherd. Jesus said that all who really loved God would love Him, too. They would know His voice, for He would be no stranger, but the true Shepherd of their souls. And because they knew His voice as the true voice of God they would follow Him. They would gladly do as He told them, and He would care for them, and help them on their journey through life.

Because He was the Good Shepherd, Jesus said He would lay down His life for the sheep. For the greatest enemy of the sheep was the Evil One who always tried to destroy the sheep by making them stray into the ways of sin. Jesus died on the Cross to destroy the works of the Evil One.

Jesus said, too, " *And other sheep I have which are not of this fold: them also I must bring, and they shall hear My voice; and there shall be one flock, and one shepherd.*"

That is coming true to-day. All over the world, men and

women, boys and girls of every nation under the sun are hearing the voice of the Good Shepherd, and following Him. All barriers are being broken down; they are all coming into the one fold, and all love one another because they all love the Good Shepherd.

The Sheep that was Lost

Nobody liked Zacchaeus. He was a very rich man, but they did not like the way he earned his money. He gathered in the taxes and the Jewish people were taxed so heavily that life was hard for them.

Not only that, the taxes Zacchaeus wrung out of them were for the hated Romans; and, to make things even worse, Zacchaeus always demanded more than he was entitled to ask for. So everybody shunned him and left him alone.

When he heard that Jesus was passing near his house, Zacchaeus made up his mind to see Him. He was a very little man and when Jesus came along he couldn't see Jesus at all for the crowd. But he wasn't at a loss, for he ran on ahead and climbed up a sycamore tree, just like a boy.

When Jesus came to the tree, He looked up, and said, "Zacchaeus, be quick and come down; for to-day I must stay at your house." Zacchaeus was so thrilled when he heard what Jesus said that he slid down that sycamore tree like lightning!

When the other Jews saw that Jesus had gone into Zacchaeus' house, they sneered. "He's gone to be the guest of a man who is a sinner!"

So Jesus told them a story. A shepherd had a flock of one hundred sheep. One night, as he was putting them into the fold, he counted them. He counted up to "ninety-seven, ninety-eight, ninety-nine, one——"—there was one short!

Quickly, he shut in the ninety-nine sheep by building up a great pile of thorns in the entrance to the fold, so that no wild animal could get in. Then he hurried off to find the lost sheep.

He did not say to himself, "I have ninety and nine sheep: why bother about one silly little sheep?" No, he went out over hill and dale, over crag, moor, and fen, searching here, there, and everywhere.

At last, there it was! The poor little thing had got itself into a difficult place and was too exhausted to climb out of it. If the shepherd had not found it, it would surely have died.

The shepherd ran forward, picked it up, swung it across his shoulders and carried it home. As he came near to his own house, he shouted out to all his neighbours: "Rejoice with me, for I have found the sheep that was lost."

When they blamed Him for having anything to do with the despised tax-gatherer, Jesus said to them, "This day is salvation come to this house—for the Son of Man is come to seek that which was lost."

Jesus was the Good Shepherd, and Zacchaeus was the sheep that was lost. He was now restored into the family of Israel and was no longer an outcaste. "Behold, Lord," he said to Jesus, "half of my goods I give to the poor; and if I have taken anything from any man wrongfully, I will restore it to him four times over."

~~~~~~

The Son Who was Lost

Jesus was the greatest teller of stories the world has ever known. And the finest story He ever told was the story we call the Story of the Prodigal Son.

A wealthy landowner had two sons. One day the younger son came to his father and said: "Father, give me now my share of the property." So the father reckoned up the value of the estate, and gave him his portion.

The young man changed everything into cash, and, leaving the old home, travelled to a foreign country. There he had a wild time, throwing his money about in all kinds of foolish ways. Many people, men and women, helped him to spend his money, and in time it was all gone—and gone too were his friends!

Just then a very bad famine occurred in that country, and the young man found himself in great difficulties. He had no food, no friends, no home, and no nice clothes. Once a rich man's son, he was now a beggar. He went to a citizen of that land, and begged for work to earn some bread, and that man sent him into the fields to feed pigs!

Now he was a swineherd, and one good thing his new job did for him—it gave him plenty of time to think. But he was so hungry that many a time he could have eaten the pigs' food. Nobody would help him or give him anything.

Once, when he was sitting so miserable beside the swine-trough, he took a thought to himself. "Here am I," he said, "feeding pigs, and I don't know how many hired servants my father has who can have all the bread they want, and more, while I am likely to die here of hunger."

"I will arise," he declared to himself, "and go to my father, and I will say to him, Father, I have sinned against God and you. I do not deserve to be called your son: make me one of your hired servants." So he set out to return to his father's house.

All the time he had been away, his father had never given up hope that his foolish boy would one day come back again, and he kept looking down the long road leading to the house, hoping that one day his younger son would be on it.

One glad morning he saw his son away in the distance, before his son saw him, and he ran down the road towards the poor, broken lad. When he came up to him, he took him in his arms and kissed him.

"Father," said the boy, "I have sinned against God and you, and am no more worthy to be called your son . . ."

But he got no further. "Bring forth the best robe, and put it on him," the father called to the servants; "and put a ring on his hand, and shoes on his feet: bring the fatted calf, and kill it; and let us eat, and be merry: for this my son was dead, and is alive again: he was lost, and is found." And they began to be merry.

The ring, and the robe, and the shoes were signs of son-

The Prodigal Son becomes a swineherd.

ship. The servants wore no rings, or robes or shoes. And the "fatted calf" was the calf that was specially fattened up to be eaten on special occasions, just as we fatten geese and turkeys for Christmas.

Now, the elder son was out working in the field, and when he had finished work, and was coming near the house, he was surprised to hear music and dancing. He called one of the servants and asked what all the singing and dancing was about, and the servant told him, "Your brother is home again; and your father has killed the fatted calf, because he has received him back safe and sound."

The elder brother was very angry, and refused to go into the house or take part in all the rejoicing. So his father came out to him, and pleaded with him to join them inside, but he still remained sulky.

He said to his father, "Look, I have served you all these years. Never once have I displeased you, and you never gave me as much as a kid to make merry with my friends. And yet, as soon as this your other son has come back, after wasting all your money on his wild pleasures, you will kill the fatted calf for him."

But the father said very gently, "Son, you have always been with me. I never lost *you*, and all I have is yours. It was only right that we should make merry and be glad; for your brother was dead and is alive again; and was lost and is found."

This story has been called "The Story of the Prodigal Son". But it would be truer to call it "The Story of the Prodigal Son's Father". For this is the third of the three stories which Jesus told to show how God cares for each one of us.

Probably most people would have thought as the elder brother did—let the foolish boy take the consequences of his wicked behaviour. But the father saw it all very differently. This foolish boy was still his son, and he still loved him, and still wanted him back into the family circle. That, said Jesus, is how God welcomes everyone who realizes how foolish he has been, and is sorry for it all.

The Good and Faithful Servant

A certain nobleman had to go on a far journey. He sent for his servants, and said to them, "I shall be away for a long time. While I am absent, I want you to look after my property for me, and carry on my work just as if I were here myself."

To one servant he gave a large sum of money, about £1,000. To another, £500, and to a third £250, according to their ability.

The first servant traded with his £1,000 and made it into £2,000. The second servant made his £500 into £1,000, but the third did a very strange thing. He took his £250 and buried it in the ground! There, of course, it was of no use to anyone.

The nobleman was away for a long time, and when he came back he sent for his servants again and asked them to account for the money he had given to them.

The first servant said, "Sir, you gave me £1,000; see, I have gained another £1,000 with it."

The nobleman was very pleased. "Well done, good and faithful servant!" he said. "You have been faithful in one thing. I will make you ruler over many things. Come, share in your master's feast of joy."

The second servant came forward. "Sir," he said, "you gave me £500. I have gained another £500 with it."

"Well done, good and faithful servant!" said the nobleman. "You have been faithful in one thing. I will make you ruler over many things. Come, share in your master's feast of joy."

The third servant then came forward. "Master," he said, "I knew you were a hard man, expecting full value for your money, and I was afraid. So I went and hid the money in the earth. See, here you have your money back again."

The nobleman answered him, "You bad, lazy servant. When you knew I expected full value for my money, why did you not lend the money to someone? I would then at least have got my money back with interest."

"Take the money from him," continued his master, "and give it to the servant who had £1,000."

This is one of the many parables which Jesus told to show how the kingdom of God may spread throughout the world.

The nobleman gives money to his three servants.

The advancement of the Kingdom depends on the faithfulness and courage of each one of us.

Just as the nobleman went away, and trusted his servants to carry on his work for him in his absence, so does the Lord Jesus trust those who love Him to carry on His work in this world. He does not ask us to be successful servants, but good and faithful servants. Our true success lies in pleasing Him.

The Story of the Sower

Great crowds gathered to hear the wonderful parables told by Jesus. On one occasion, down by the seaside, the crowd was so large that Jesus had to speak from a boat in the sea to the people sitting on the shore. Perhaps, away in the distance, Jesus could see a farmer sowing his field, and it was this that led Him to tell this story of the Sower and the Seed.

A sower went out to sow, and as he sowed some seed fell on the hard path running along by the side of the field, and the birds came and ate the seed all up.

Some of the seed fell on ground where there was more stone than soil. It grew up quickly for the soil was very shallow, and the hot sun scorched and withered it, because it did not have enough root.

Other seed fell among thorns, and as it grew up the thorns grew still more quickly and choked the wheat, and so there was no grain from it.

Yet other seed fell on good ground, and it came up and increased splendidly so that some of it yielded thirty, sixty, and some even a hundredfold as much.

Later on in the day, when He was sitting with His twelve disciples, probably having a meal together, they asked Jesus to tell them the meaning of the Parable of the Sower and the Seed.

Jesus explained that the Sower in the parable is the man who gives to others the Word of God, and the Word of God is the seed which he sows in their hearts.

The seed that fell on the path trodden hard by the feet of the passers-by is like those people who hear the Word of God but do not allow it to sink into their hearts. They hear it but before they can really understand what it means, they forget all about it in thinking of other things—just as birds snatch away the good seed before it can begin to grow.

The seed that fell on the stony soil is like the shallow-minded people who hear the Word of God and accept it with great enthusiasm to start with. But it takes no root in their hearts, and, when trouble or persecution comes along, they are easily discouraged, and they give it up.

The third kind of seed—the kind that fell among thorns, is like those who hear the Word and try at first to put it into practice in their daily lives. But very soon other interests come crowding into their lives—cares and worries, business and pleasures, and all their good intentions are simply crowded out. There is no time or inclination to listen any more to God's Word.

But the fourth kind of seed is very different. It is like those who hear the Word of God and welcome it into their hearts. As they read about Jesus, they want to be like Him, and all who know them see how good and kind they are becoming. It is like watching the good seed growing into a rich and lovely harvest.

"As We Forgive"

One day, Peter came to Jesus and asked him, "Lord, how many times should I forgive anyone who does me an unkind thing? Seven times?" Peter, no doubt, thought that seven times were more than enough to go on forgiving any one.

But Jesus replied, "I would say not seven times, but seventy times seven!" And then to show that He really meant what He said, Jesus went on to tell a story.

Once upon a time, there was a King who decided to have a reckoning with his servants. He discovered that one of them actually owed him between two and three million pounds.

He sent for this man and demanded immediate payment of this huge amount. When the servant said he had no money to pay, the King ordered that everything he had was to be sold to help pay the debt, including the man himself, his wife, and his children.

The servant fell down on his knees before the King and pleaded for time to pay the debt. "Have patience with me," he implored, "and I will pay it all back to you."

The King saw that the man could not possibly pay such a large sum, no matter how long he was given, and he felt very sorry for him, so he decided to forgive him the debt altogether. The man was therefore set free.

When he was leaving the palace, he met one of his fellow-servants who owed him about ten pounds. He caught this other servant by the throat and said, "Pay me the debt you owe me!"

His fellow-servant fell on his knees before him, and pleaded with him, "Have patience with me, and I will pay you all." But he refused to wait, and had his fellow-servant arrested and put into a debtors' prison.

Now, the other servants were very upset about this behaviour, and they went and told the King what had happened. The King was so angry when he heard this that he sent again for the man, and said to him, "You wicked servant! I forgave you all that great debt when you implored me to have pity on you. Ought you not to have taken pity on your fellow-servant in the same way, and to have forgiven him his very small debt?"

And, because he was so indignant at such base ingratitude, the King ordered the unforgiving servant to be handed over to those who would punish him until his great debt was paid and the matter put right.

At the end of this sad story, Jesus added this grave warning, "My Heavenly Father will do the same to you, if you do not from your hearts forgive those who have offended you."

Jesus simply meant that since we owe so much to God for all His love to us, we ought to be kind and understanding with others, even to those who are unkind to us. If we allow ourselves to have an ungracious, unforgiving nature, we will never know the peace and happiness of God's forgiveness and friendship for ourselves.

The Pearl of Great Price

Jesus once told two tiny little stories to teach a very great lesson.

The first story was about a man who found a valuable treasure trove in a field. Perhaps he was ploughing, and, as so often happens, even in our own country, the plough-share turned the treasure up out of the place where it had been carefully hidden.

Now, at that time, "finders" could be "keepers", so the man hastily covered the treasure up again. He was so thrilled by this discovery of sudden wealth, and the dazzling prospect it opened up to him, that he sold everything he possessed, and with the money went and bought the field. In this way he became the owner of the field and everything in it, including the treasure.

The second story concerned a pearl merchant who travelled great distances looking for pearls of the purest quality. One day he came across a pearl which seemed to answer all his fondest dreams of what a pearl should be like.

Immediately he went and sold all he possessed, including, no doubt, all the other pearls he had previously bought, in order to buy this wonderful pearl he had so unexpectedly discovered.

What was the lesson which Jesus was anxious to teach His disciples when He told them these two precious little stories? It was this, when a person has had a glimpse of what the Kingdom of Heaven is really like; when he sees how good it would be to live in that Kingdom and make it known to others so that all might share in its beauty and happiness, he will be prepared to surrender everything for its sake, if that should be necessary.

Thousands upon thousands of people have done just that. St. Francis of Assisi, for example, was one. The Apostle Paul was another, and he spoke for them all when he said, "What things were gain to me I counted as loss for the sake of Christ. Yes, and I count everything well lost when compared with

THE RICH FOOL

the priceless joy of knowing Christ Jesus, my Lord. For His
sake I suffered the loss of all things, and regard them as rub-
bish so long as I have Christ as my friend."

~~~~~~

The Rich Fool

There was once a rich man who had several farms. He had
been very prosperous, but one year his harvest broke all
records. As he looked across his broad fields, laden with
grain, his only concern was what he was going to do with it
all and where he should store it.

He thought to himself, "What shall I do, because I have
no space where I can put all my crops. I know what I'll do,
I'll pull down my barns, and build larger barns, and there I
will keep all my grain and all my goods."

Then he said something else to himself. "And I will say to
my soul, Soul, you have enough stored up for the rest of
your life. Now, have a good time : take your comfort; eat,
drink, and be merry."

But God said to him, "You foolish man, this very night you
will die; then whose will all those things be that you have
stored up?"

"That is what happens," said Jesus, as He finished this
story, "to the man who makes himself rich, but not with the
true riches that comes from trusting in God."

This man was not a fool because he became rich. Indeed,
he must have been very clever to have prospered so well.
But where he was foolish was in forgetting that money cannot buy the best things in life. Those things God *gives* to
those who love Him.

The rich man also forgot that while his body might die at
any time, his soul would never die but live for ever, and in
that other world where earthly riches have no value; where
what counts is not what a man has but what a man is.

Jesus told His disciples that they were not to keep on worrying about how they were going to live, about the kind of food they would eat, or the kind of clothes they would wear.

"Think of the birds," said Jesus. "They do not sow and reap and build barns. God takes care of them. Consider the lilies. They do not toil and spin, and yet God gives them such lovely dresses that Solomon in all his glory was not arrayed like one of them."

Jesus did not mean we were not to think of these things at all. But we are not to think of them as the most important things in life. "*Seek ye first the Kingdom of God,*" He said, "*and all these things will be added unto you.*"

The first and most important thing is to seek to please God in everything we do, and help others to do the same, so that God's will is done on the earth as it is done in heaven.

That, said Jesus, is the true coin of God's realm. It is like putting treasure in the Bank of Heaven. Thieves cannot steal that kind of treasure. It never becomes tarnished with time. That is how to be rich towards God, "*For where your treasure is, there will your heart be also.*"

The Sermon on the Mount

Jesus did nearly all of His teaching in the open air. The crowds that followed Jesus were so great that no building could ever have held them all. But that was not the only reason. Jesus loved to be in the open. With the blue sky above and the green grass beneath, He loved to teach the people.

It must have been a wonderful sight to see those great crowds, dressed in the bright colours of the East, jostling and pushing one another, talking and gesticulating, as they waited for the Teacher to speak.

Then a deep silence would fall over the great throng as
Jesus began to say those wonderful words which have brought
life and health and peace to countless numbers then and
since.

One day, Jesus climbed a mountainside. He sat on a little
hillock, and the great crowd of people spread themselves in a
huge semicircle below Him. Nearer to Him were His own
disciples, and Jesus began what has been called ever since
the Sermon on the Mount.

The Sermon begins with nine Beatitudes. A Beatitude is
really a secret of true happiness, and here we have nine such
secrets. They all start with the word "Blessed" which
means "Most happy are you". Each secret has a condition
attached to it, because before we can know what true happiness means, there are certain conditions to be fulfilled.

You may think that some of the conditions are very hard.
But let us read the Beatitudes first, and come back to that
point again.

Blessed are the poor in spirit:
    for theirs is the kingdom of heaven.
Blessed are they that mourn:
    for they shall be comforted.
Blessed are the meek:
    for they shall inherit the earth.
Blessed are they which do hunger and thirst after
    righteousness: for they shall be filled.
Blessed are the merciful:
    for they shall obtain mercy.
Blessed are the pure in heart:
    for they shall see God.
Blessed are the peacemakers:
    for they shall be called the children of God.
Blessed are they which are persecuted for righteousness'
    sake: for theirs is the kingdom of heaven.
Blessed are you when men shall revile and persecute you,
    and shall say all manner of evil against you falsely for
    my sake.

Rejoice and be exceeding glad: for great is your reward in heaven: for so persecuted they the prophets which were before you.

Now that you have read the Beatitudes, you will agree that they are not the kind of secrets that people usually call happy secrets. But we do agree, do we not, that if everybody were really gentle in spirit, humble in heart, and eager only for the right things, and always prepared to suffer and even to die for them, the world would be a happier place?

The trouble is, of course, that nearly everybody is waiting on everybody else to make a beginning. Well, Jesus has made a beginning. He is the Leader and many have followed Him. They are the members of His Kingdom, and the Beatitudes are the laws of that Kingdom which, with His help, they endeavour to obey. When enough people in the world do the same, then that Kingdom will really come, and all that is wrong be done away with for ever.

Going the Second Mile

In the days when Jesus walked the lanes of Palestine, the little country was occupied by the Romans. Although the Romans allowed the Jews many liberties, especially in regard to their religion, there were many things that irritated and annoyed the Jews and made them hate the Romans with a bitter hatred.

Here, for example, was one way by which the Romans made themselves very unpopular with the ordinary Jew. A Roman soldier is marching along the road with a heavy pack. He sees a Jew coming along, and he says to him, "Here, you! Carry this pack a mile for me." The Jew has to do it, for the Roman soldier could force him. But he does it with hatred for the Roman in his heart.

Jesus said, "If a man compels you to go a mile, go with him two."

The world into which Jesus came was a world full of hatred and quarrelling. People spiting one another, taking one another to court, and compelling one another to do unpleasant things.

It was a vicious circle, everybody wanting to get "their own back". Jesus said that circle must be broken, if the

A Roman soldier compels a Jew to carry his pack.

world is to have peace. And He says to each one of His followers, "Let the flow of hatred stop at you—don't let it go any farther. Always be generous; never grudging."

We have a proverb "Revenge is sweet". But Jesus says there must be none of that in His Kingdom, for revenge is not sweet at all. It only brings bitterness and more hatred.

Those who love Jesus and want to please Him are not to meet evil with evil but to overcome evil with good. That is not to be a coward. No one would ever think of Jesus as

185

a coward. In the Judgment Hall of Pilate they mocked Him, but He remained silent. As He hung on the Cross, men reviled Him, but He reviled not again. He prayed, "Father, forgive them, they know not what they do."

Jesus hated all the cheating and lying, cruelty and wickedness in the world, but He did not go about hitting back at people all the time. He went about doing good. He healed the sick, comforted the sad, raised up the fallen, and helped people to be good and kind.

"*Love your enemies,*" said Jesus, "*bless them that curse you, do good to them that hate you, and pray for them which despitefully use you, and persecute you; that ye may be the children of your Father which is in heaven: for He maketh His sun to rise on the evil and on the good, and sendeth rain on the just and on the unjust.*"

After all, said Jesus, if you love those who love you, and do good to those who do good to you, anybody can do that. But when we love those who hate us, and do good to those who want to harm us, then we shall be like God Himself, Who loves all men everywhere, good and bad alike.

When You Pray

There was one thing, above all else, that Jesus warned people to be on their guard against—hypocrisy.

A hypocrite is one who would like everybody to think he is a good person while really at heart he is a bad one.

Jesus gave two examples of this kind of hypocrisy. There was the man who was going to give a donation to the poor, or, perhaps, to the church. He hired a trumpeter to sound a flourish on his trumpet, and then when a crowd had gathered round, he put his donation into the box. But, said Jesus, when you want to give to charity, "*let not your left hand know what your right hand is doing*".

186

The second example was the man who loved to pray long prayers standing up in the synagogue, or even at the corner of the street. He wanted to hear people say, "What a good man that is!"

"But," Jesus said, "when you pray, go into your own room, and when you have shut the door, pray to your heavenly Father who is in secret; and your Father who sees in secret, will himself reward you openly."

The people who do good just to be seen of men have their reward. They get what they want—public applause. But the people who do good not to be seen of men but to be seen of God have a different kind of reward. It is the "open reward" of a happy face, because they have a happy and peaceful heart.

Jesus also told the story of "The Pharisee and the Publican". The Pharisee came striding into the Temple one day to pray. His prayer was one long hymn of praise—to himself. He reminded God of the fine man he was: he went to Church regularly; he gave a lot of money away, and he was very respectable. He thanked God he was not like other men who were not respectable. Then, noticing a man standing behind him, he finished his prayer like this: "I thank you, God, I am not like this publican."

Now the publican, or tax-gatherer, was not proud or boastful. He did not even lift up his eyes, but smote his breast, and said very humbly, "God be merciful to me a sinner."

"I tell you," said Jesus, as He finished this story. "It was not the Pharisee, but the publican who returned home with peace in his heart."

Do not think, said Jesus, that God only hears long prayers. He hears the simple, sincere prayers of humble people. And our Lord gave us a pattern prayer to show us what He meant. We call it "The Lord's Prayer".

> *Our Father which art in heaven,*
> *Hallowed be thy name.*
> *Thy kingdom come.*
> *Thy will be done in earth, as it is in heaven.*

Give us this day our daily bread.
And forgive us our debts,
  as we forgive our debtors.
And lead us not into temptation,
  but deliver us from evil:
For thine is the kingdom, and the power,
  and the glory, for ever.
                              Amen.

The Fault-finders

Another thing that made Jesus very angry was the way people judged and criticized one another. On one occasion, some very religious Jews dragged a poor woman before Jesus. They said she had done something very wicked, and that, according to the law, she should be put to death by stoning.

Jesus said to them, "He that is without sin among you, let him cast the first stone." And He then bent down, and began to write with His finger in the sand.

When He looked up again, all the men were gone! Only the woman was left. "Where are all your accusers?" Jesus asked. "Does no man condemn you?"

"No man, Lord," the poor woman said.

"Neither do I condemn you," Jesus said gently to her. "Go and sin no more."

"Judge not that you be not judged," Jesus said to His disciples, in the Sermon on the Mount. "For with what judgment you judge others, you will yourselves be judged; and the justice you measure out to others will be the justice that will be measured out to you."

Then He drew for them a word-picture; or what we would call to-day a caricature.

One man said to another, "You've got a speck of wood in your eye. Let me take it out for you."

188

But, said Jesus, "that same man had a whole log of wood sticking out of his own eye."

No doubt, the disciples would smile at this picture of one man, with a whole beam sticking out of his own eye, trying to take a tiny speck out of the eye of someone else.

But that is just like the person who goes about fault-finding, said Jesus. "You hypocrite, first cast out the beam out of your own eye; and then you will see clearly to cast the mote out of your friend's eye."

The Wonderful Secret

We all love to read about the fairy secret that changes everything—sadness into joy, poverty into wealth, sickness into health, ugliness into beauty. Alas! they are only fairy stories which leave the world as it was before.

But Jesus gives us a new secret which, if men used it truly and sincerely, would change the world and everybody in it. This is the secret—"All things whatsoever you would like others to do to you, do you even so to them: for this is the law and the prophets." The secret has been called "The Golden Rule". And what a lovely thing it would be if we all tried to carry it out!

For example, we see, or hear of, someone in some need. We say to ourselves, "Now, if I were that person and he were me, what would I like him to do for me? How would I feel if I were in his place?" To ask a question like that, said Jesus, is to know the answer. We should do all we can to help that person.

But, if we are honest with ourselves, we know we are not like that. We are not often ready to see the other person's position, and to think out how best we can help him. Before we can apply the *secret* of Jesus, we need to have the *Spirit* of Jesus.

189

But the Spirit of Jesus is not something we can work up like enthusiasm for some good cause. It is a gift which only our heavenly Father can give us. And Jesus tells us that our Father in Heaven will give us this precious gift, if we ask Him for it with the true and earnest desire to be His loving children.

No earthly father would ever refuse his child a good gift when that child comes to him in loving trust and obedience. In Palestine, the common food of the peasant people was bread and fish. The bread was baked in small round loaves, not unlike little round stones. Some fishes looked very like little serpents. Now, said Jesus, when a little boy asks for bread, his father does not give him a stone. When he asks his father for a fish, he does not give him a serpent. He loves his boy too much to play any such tricks on him.

"Well," said Jesus, "if an earthly father knows how to give good gifts to his children; how much more will our Heavenly Father give good gifts to them that ask Him." And the best gift even God can give us is the Spirit of His dear Son our Saviour.

The Poor Woman and the Rich Girl

In a little town by the Sea of Galilee there lived a rich ruler called Jairus. He was the chief man in the synagogue, and was respected by all the people. But his greatest joy was his little girl who was only twelve.

Suddenly the little girl took very ill, and Jairus thought she was likely to die. In his great anxiety, he thought of Jesus.

He had heard of the wonderful works of mercy Jesus had been doing elsewhere so he hurried to where Jesus was, and, great man though he was, he fell down at the Saviour's feet and besought Him to come and heal his only child.

Jesus set out to go with him to where the girl was lying so ill at home. But their progress was very slow, because a great crowd was following them, pressing round on every side, so that there was hardly room to move.

In that crowd was a poor woman who had been very ill for many years. She had been well-off once and had spent all her money on doctors and medicines, but was worse instead of better, and now poor as well.

She too had heard of Jesus, and was determined to see Him. Some people think her name was Veronica and that she lived in Caesarea Phillipi. If so, she would have had to travel quite a good distance.

She pressed her way through the crowd, and squeezed in behind Jesus. "If only I can touch the hem of His garment," she had said to herself, "I shall be made well again."

She put her hand out very timidly and touched one of the tassels on the fringe of Jesus' cloak, and immediately she felt cured of the dreadful illness that had plagued her for many years. As soon as she touched Him, Jesus stood still. "Who touched Me?" He exclaimed.

Everybody declared they had not touched Him, and Peter said, "Master, this great crowd is thronging and pressing all around, and yet You ask who touched You!"

"Somebody has deliberately touched Me," said Jesus, "for I knew at once that power had gone out from Me."

The poor woman saw that what she had done had not gone unnoticed, so she came forward trembling, and fell at the feet of Jesus in the centre of the crowd. She told Jesus all about herself. How she had been so ill for so long, and had spent all her money on doctors and medicines but was worse instead of better. How she had come all the way, not meaning to trouble Jesus, but just to touch the hem of His garment. How she had done so and had felt quite well again.

Jesus looked down at her, and said, "Daughter, do not be afraid, your faith has made you whole. Go home again in peace."

Just then a messenger came from the house of Jairus, and said to him, "Your daughter is dead: there is no need now to trouble the Master."

But when Jesus heard that, He said to Jairus, "Fear not; only believe, and your daughter will be made quite well."

When they came to the house of Jairus, they heard there a terrible hubbub going on. In the East, it is sometimes the custom to hire professional mourners—people who dress up in sad-looking clothes and make a loud wailing and moaning noise in the house and during the funeral procession.

Jesus restores Jairus's daughter to life.

Jesus said to them, "Why do you make such a noise? You don't need to weep and wail like that. She is not dead, only sleeping."

But they all laughed Him to scorn, for they knew the girl was dead. He put them all out of the room, and took with Him only Peter, James, and John, and the father and mother of the girl.

Jesus went up to where the girl was lying, so pale and still. He took her by the hand, and said quietly to her, "Little girl, get up!" Just as her mother must have said to her often when she wakened her in the morning. The girl opened her eyes and looked at Jesus as He smiled down at her, and I am sure she smiled back at Him.

Then Jesus gave her to her father and mother, and said, "Now, give her something to eat."

Jairus and his wife were amazed and overwhelmed with gratitude to Jesus Who had raised their little daughter from the dead. But Jesus told them they were not to tell anybody about it. They were to keep what He had done as a little family secret.

We do not know the little girl's name, but we may be certain she never forgot how when she opened her eyes from that long, strange sleep, the first thing she saw was the smiling face of Jesus.

The Blind Beggar

Sitting by the roadside, just outside the city of Jericho, was a blind man called Bartimæus. He was well known to the people who came in and out of the city, for he had been there begging for almost as long as anyone could remember.

Bartimæus knew all the familiar sounds of the traffic that passed by where he sat day after day. But one day he heard a sound that he had never heard before. It was the noise of a great crowd of people, buzzing with excitement. The blind man asked what was happening, and someone told him that Jesus of Nazareth was passing by.

Now, a blind man cannot see but he often does a great deal more thinking than most people who can see. And as Bartimæus sat there by the roadside, he thought a lot about the strange rumours that were being passed about from mouth to mouth.

People were talking about a Jesus from Nazareth who was making blind people to see, deaf people to hear, dumb people to speak, and lame people to walk.

Many blind people have remarkable memories, and it may well be that Bartimæus had stored in his mind the Scriptures he had heard the minister read in the synagogue. As he sat there in the sun, he pondered over what he had heard, and something of their meaning became clearer and clearer to him. Especially those Scriptures which spoke of the coming of the King Who would give sight to those who were blind.

So, as he heard those stories about this wonder-working Jesus of Nazareth, he wished earnestly that he could go to where Jesus was so that he could prove for himself whether this was indeed the promised King. And now this Jesus of Nazareth was actually passing by a few feet away from him. He could not see Jesus. Was Jesus seeing him? he wondered. Anyway, here was the chance of a lifetime, and he was determined to seize it.

He shouted out at the top of his old voice. But he did not call "Jesus of Nazareth!" No, he called, "Jesus, Son of David, have mercy on me." He had now made up his mind that Jesus was no mere magician or sorcerer from Nazareth but none other than the One sent by God from Heaven, Who was able to do those wonderful things only by the power of God. "Jesus, thou Son of David, have mercy on me!" he shouted again.

People in the crowd told him to be quiet. They had come to hear the wonderful things Jesus would sometimes say to His disciples as He walked along, and they did not want the shouting of a blind old man to prevent them from hearing.

But Bartimæus shouted all the more, "Jesus, thou Son of David, have mercy on me! Jesus, thou Son of David, have mercy on me."

And Jesus stood still when He heard that cry. He stopped, and commanded Bartimæus to be brought to Him.

The crowd turned to the blind old man, and said to him, "Be of good comfort, rise up! He is calling for you."

The old man threw aside the cloak which was his beggar's badge and uniform, and sprang to his feet, and came towards Jesus.

"What do you wish Me to do for you?" Jesus asked the old man.

"Lord, that I might receive my sight!" came the reply.

"Go your way," said Jesus to him; "your faith has made you whole." Bartimæus was no longer blind. He could see. No more begging for him. The last we see of the old man is going along with the crowd that followed Jesus along the way. We may be sure he was now seeing not only with the eyes in his head, but also with the eyes in his heart. For in his heart he knew that the One Who had given him sight was none other than the promised Saviour.

~~~~~~

Helping Jesus to Work a Miracle

One sunny morning in Palestine, nearly 2,000 years ago, a little boy said to his mother, "Mother, Jesus of Nazareth is in the district, and I want to see and hear Him."

His mother was very good and very wise. She did not discourage him, but she remembered what he, in his excitement, had probably forgotten, that he would be away all day and would get very hungry. So she made up a little picnic lunch for him of five small barley loaves and two small fishes she had cooked. And off the boy went as happy as a king.

When he got near to the place where Jesus was, he found himself in a dense crowd. Everybody seemed to be on his way to see and hear Jesus. Men and women, boys and girls, all out for the day like himself. But not many had been so thoughtful as his mother had been. He did not see any others carrying picnic-lunches! Our little boy pushed his way through the crowd till he found himself quite near the centre where Jesus was.

There was Peter and James and John and Philip. And, yes, he could see Andrew, Peter's brother. He knew them quite well. Many a time he had watched them while they were fishing or mending their nets. That was before they had left everything to follow Jesus.

195

Andrew recognized him, and grinned a welcome, and the boy held up his little packet of food to show he meant to make a day of it.

The hot day wore on and so spellbound was the great crowd, as they listened to the words of Jesus, that no one seems to have thought about food.

But Jesus was thinking about it. As He looked over that great crowd of people, He was full of compassion for them. They looked like a great flock of sheep without a shepherd to care for them.

Deceived and cheated by their own religious leaders, and cruelly oppressed by those hated foreigners, the Romans, they were looking to Him for guidance and leadership.

And now the day was drawing to a close, and all these people were still there, unwilling to go home. Some of His disciples came to Jesus and said to Him, "This is a desert place, and the evening is coming on. Send this great crowd into the villages so that they can buy food for themselves."

Jesus said to them, "They need not go away. *You* give them food." And then, turning to Philip, He continued, "Where shall we buy bread that all these may eat?"

Jesus asked this, not because He did not know the answer Himself, but just to see how Philip would handle the situation.

Poor Philip was all flustered. "Why, two hundred penny-worth of bread would not be enough to feed all that crowd!" he exclaimed. A penny was a day's wage for a labourer in the fields, and two hundred pennies seemed a lot of money to Philip—far more than they had amongst them all.

Andrew then said, "There is a lad here who has five barley loaves and two small fishes; but what are they among so many?"

But Jesus quietly said, "Make the people sit down in rows." And the great crowd of more than five thousand men, not counting the women and children, sat down like some great picnic party.

Jesus then took the five little loaves and the two small fishes from the little lad. He said grace over them, thanking God for this food. Then He distributed the loaves and the

Andrew brings to Jesus the boy with the loaves and fishes.

fishes to His twelve disciples, and they went up and down the rows of hungry people, handing food to them.

They kept on giving out the food and it never became exhausted in their hands, until everyone in that big crowd had had enough, and could not possibly eat a scrap more.

When they had all finished eating, Jesus said to His disciples, "Gather up the fragments that remain, that nothing be lost." And the disciples gathered up twelve basketfuls of the fragments left over from this wonderful feast.

When the little lad returned home that night, he probably burst into the house with great excitement, shouting, "Mummy, Jesus and I worked a great miracle to-day!"

And he would have been quite right. No doubt Jesus could have done this great miracle without the little boy's help, but the fact is He did not.

That kind of miracle has happened again and again many times since. Jesus has taken the little offering of some man or woman, or even of some boy or girl, and has multiplied it many, many times over.

The Man With Four Friends

One time after Jesus had been teaching and healing in different places in the district, He came back to Capernaum, and was staying probably in the house of Peter.

But there was no rest for Jesus. As soon as it was known that He was back, people crowded to Peter's house, including a number of leading Pharisees and teachers of the law, who had come to examine this new teaching that had been causing such a stir. The crowd pressed right into the house, and filled the little courtyard outside.

Now, in Capernaum there was a man who was, the Bible says, "sick of the palsy". Probably this was some kind of paralysis, for the man could not walk but lay helpless.

I am afraid his illness had been caused by some sinful habit, and now the poor man was lying powerless, feeling very unhappy and full of regret. Fortunately, he had four friends. There must have been something very likeable about the man when four friends came regularly to see him, sometimes all at once.

One day, when the five friends were all together, one of them said, "I hear Jesus is back again."

"Yes," said another, looking at their sick friend lying there on the floor on his mat-bed, "and you should see the crowds of sick people who find their way wherever Jesus comes or goes."

"Pity you couldn't get there," said the third friend to the sick man.

"Why not?" said the fourth. "Where there's a will there's a way!"

"Oh, if only I could," said the paralysed man. "But how?" he sighed.

"I tell you what," replied the fourth friend. "Let's each take a corner of the bed, and carry him to Jesus."

"What a great idea!" said the other. "Why didn't we think of that before?"

So, before the man had time to think, his friends each took a corner of his bed, and carried it down the street like a stretcher. Soon they came to Peter's house. "Where are you going with that?" asked one of the bystanders.

"We are taking our friend to Jesus to be healed," they replied.

"You'll never get in; the place is simply crammed to the courtyard gate," was the disappointing reply.

They laid the bed gently down on the ground, and held a council to discuss what they should do next. The fourth man, who was full of ideas, suddenly said, "Look here, if only we can get the bed up those stairs on to the roof, we could make a hole in the roof and let our friend down just where Jesus is in the house."

"Peter might not like you knocking holes in his roof," said one of the others.

"Oh, I don't know," replied the fourth friend. "Peter is a good fellow, and, anyway, it won't be a hard job repairing his roof again."

The roofs in Palestine were flat and made simply of laths criss-crossed, covered over with brushwood, and then plastered over with clay which was dried hard by the sun.

The sick man is lowered through the roof in front of Jesus.

The four friends picked up the bed again, pushed their way through the crowd in the courtyard, and climbed the stair to the roof. They then opened up the roof very carefully. Perhaps one of them was a plasterer himself and knew how to do it. Then they took the ropes they had tied to the four corners of the bed, and slowly lowered it till it rested on the ground right at the feet of Jesus.

They did not need to say a word. When Jesus looked up

and saw the four earnest faces looking down at Him, and then looked at the paralysed man, He realized what they wanted Him to do.

Jesus was delighted by the whole business. This was the kind of thing He was trying to teach people to do—to help one another in need.

The poor paralysed man was not feeling so optimistic as his friends were. In the presence of Jesus, he realized that he had not been a good man in the past. He had brought this trouble on himself, and if Jesus did not, or could not, heal him, there was nobody to blame but himself.

But Jesus said to him, "Courage, son! your sins are all forgiven."

Well, that was good news, even if nothing more happened. To know his sins were forgiven was like a heavy weight off his heart.

The Pharisees and the teachers of the law, who were sitting there watching all this, started whispering to one another, "Why does this man speak blasphemies? Who can forgive sins but God only?"

Now, Jesus knew what they were thinking, and He spoke sharply to them. "Why do you go on arguing with yourselves," He said to them. "You think it is easy to say 'Your sins are forgiven you'. Which is easier to say to this sick man—'your sins are forgiven you' or 'take up your bed and walk'?

"But that you may know that the Son of Man has power on earth to forgive sins (He then turned to the paralysed man), I say to you, Arise, and take up your bed, and go your way back to your own home."

At once, the man got up, rolled up his bed, and marched away with it under his arm, to the great astonishment of all that huge crowd.

We never hear any more about the four friends, but it is not difficult to imagine what happened. I think when they saw their friend march out of the room with his bed under his arm, they would hurry down the stairs to meet him.

When they got back to their friend's home, the five of

them would go over the whole scene, talking excitedly to one another.

" ' Arise, take up your bed and go your way,' He said. Just like that! " one of them perhaps remarked, still in a maze.

" ' Courage, son! your sins are all forgiven,' was what He said first of all," would be the thoughtful remark of the man they had all carried helpless on his bed, only an hour or so before.

~~~~~~~~~~~~~~~~~~~~~~~~~~~~~~~~~~~~~

The Man With No Friends

In many different parts of the world there are places which are said to have strange powers of healing. Crowds of pilgrims make their way there, by one means or another, in the hope of finding a cure for some disease or trouble which seems to be beyond the power of any doctors to cure.

There was such a place in Jerusalem called the Pool of Bethesda, or the Pool of the Five Porches. Every now and then, some disturbance took place in the water of the pool—probably caused by a hidden stream bubbling up from below. It was believed that this movement in the water was caused by an angel, and that the first one to plunge into the water while it was bubbling up would be cured from whatever illness troubled him.

Hundreds of people practically lived in this place—people with every kind of illness, many of them brought there by friends—all waiting for the troubling of the waters. And what a scrambling and struggling took place, the moment the waters bubbled up! each person trying to be the first to get into the water.

It is not surprising to find that Jesus visited such a place. Wherever there were people requiring to be helped, Jesus was most likely to be found. As He moved about amongst those poor people, Jesus came to a man who had become almost

202

part of the place itself, for he had been lying there for a very long time. Practically everybody in Jerusalem knew about him and had become accustomed to seeing him there day after day.

Jesus stopped before this man's bed, and said to him, "Do you really want to be whole again?"

That may seem a strange question to ask a man who had been ill for thirty-eight years and was waiting to be healed. But there are some people who enjoy being ill. They become so accustomed to the idea that they are not really interested in being anything else.

Or it may well be that the man had lost all hope of ever becoming well again, and Jesus wanted to stir up hope in the man's heart, and that is why He said, "Do you really want to be whole again?"

The man answered Him, "Sir, I have no friend, when the water is troubled, to help me into the pool: and while I am creeping down myself into the water, someone else steps down before me, and I lose my chance again."

Jesus said to him, "Rise, roll up your bed and walk from here."

Immediately, the man felt he had been made quite well, and he got to his feet, took up his mat-bed, and walked away.

All this happened on the Sabbath day, and, as he was walking out of the place, some of the Jewish authorities stopped him, and said to him, "It is the Sabbath day. It is against our law for you to be carrying your bed on the Sabbath day." The man replied, "He who made me whole told me to take up my bed and walk."

"What man told you to take up your bed and walk?" they asked him. The man could not tell them, for after He had made the man well, Jesus had mingled with the dense crowd of people, and was gone before the man could find out who He was.

Some days afterwards, Jesus was in the Temple and there He came face to face with the man whom He had healed by the pool. "Look," He said to the man, "you are made whole: do not sin any more, lest something worse should happen."

From this we may believe that the man's long illness had been the result of some sinful habit, just as in the case of the man who had four friends to bring him to Jesus for healing.

By this encounter with Jesus in the Temple, the man who had no friend to help him learned Who Jesus was. He went and told the Jewish rulers that it was Jesus Who had healed him, and had told him to take up his bed and walk.

We do not know why he did this. We can only hope that he did not know that the rulers of the Jews were now seeking an excuse to arrest Jesus. Whatever the man's reason was, from that time the Jewish authorities sought to have Jesus put to death, because He performed many of His miracles on the Sabbath day.

This man had been ill for thirty-eight years and, instead of being glad that the man was cured at all, they were angry with Jesus because He did not wait one day more.

The Touch of Jesus

One of the most dreadful and most dreaded of all diseases is the one known as leprosy. To-day, leprosy may be cured, but even now a person with leprosy must go away from other people, for a time at least, and perhaps for all time.

In olden times there was no cure, and the leper was doomed from the start. He had to hide himself from other people, and if by any chance he came near to other people, he had to call out "Unclean! Unclean!" to warn the others to keep their distance.

Not only that but if anyone touched a leper in any way, he too was regarded as a leper, until he was seen to be free from the disease. So terrified were people by the very thought of leprosy.

There used to be lepers in our own country. In some places even to-day you may see churches with little openings in the

" Rise, roll up your bed and walk from here."

walls. These were made to permit the leper to hear the service from outside the main building which he was not allowed to enter.

Just because of his pitiable state, the leper has always been a special care of those who truly love the Lord Jesus. St. Francis once kissed a leper to show that Christ loved lepers. We all know the story of Father Damien who became a leper himself, because of his work amongst the lepers. And to-day in many parts of the world Christian missionaries are caring for these poor sick folk.

Once a leper came to Jesus, kneeling before Him and pleading that Jesus would heal him. "If You will, You can make me clean," he said.

Jesus looked at the poor man, and was filled with a tender pity for him. He put out His hand and touched him. "I will," He said. "You are clean." And immediately the leprosy left the man, and he was quite healthy again.

Jesus very strictly instructed the man not to tell any person how he had been cured from the leprosy, but to go straight to the priest, and make the offering for cleansing from leprosy which was commanded in the law of Moses. The priest would then give him the necessary certificate showing he was no longer a leper.

But the man was so excited about his wonderful cure that he told everybody he met! Perhaps, too, he was so proud that he could now call attention to himself, instead of having to avoid people and to drive them away from him.

The result was that for a long time Jesus could not show Himself in the crowded cities, but had to stay in the desert. If people wanted to hear him—and thousands did—they had to go into the desert place where Jesus was. You see, by touching the leper Jesus had legally made Himself a leper, and so, according to the law, He had to remain isolated for a while.

How like our kind Saviour to touch a leper! His love did not stop to think of the possible consequences to Himself. He always enters in this way into the sufferings of others.

Matthew tells us of one marvellous day in the life of Jesus

—"and when even was come, they brought to Him many that were possessed with devils: and He cast out the spirits with His word, and healed all that were sick: that it might be fulfilled which Isaiah the prophet foretold, Himself took our infirmities, and bare our sicknesses."

A Soldier's Servant

As we have already seen, the Roman soldier was not popular in Palestine. But there was at least one Roman soldier whom everybody liked.

He was a Centurion; what we would call to-day a sergeant-major. A Centurion was in charge of a Century—a Roman company consisting of one hundred soldiers.

The Romans worshipped many gods, but this Centurion seems to have come to believe that the God of Israel was the only true and living God. He did not become a Jew, however, but he helped the Jews in Capernaum to build a synagogue. And, going about among the Jews, he seems to have heard about Jesus.

This Roman soldier must have been both good and kind, for when one of his servants became very ill, and seemed likely to die, he was very concerned about him. In his great anxiety for his servant, he thought to himself. "If only Jesus would come and heal him! But Jesus is not likely to come into the home of a Roman soldier." So he went to the elders of the Jewish synagogue, and asked them to go to Jesus on his behalf.

The elders came to Jesus and said to Him, "We have a Roman Centurion in our town who is very anxious about one of his servants who seems to be dying. He wants you to come and heal the servant, and we think he is very deserving of your sympathy. Although he is a Roman, he loves our nation, and has even built us a synagogue."

Jesus agreed at once to go with them. When they were coming near to the Centurion's house, another group of Jewish friends met them with a message from him for Jesus. "Lord, do not trouble yourself," was the message, "for I am not worthy that You should come under my roof.

"I am not even worthy to meet You myself," the message continued, "but if You will only say the word where You are, my servant will be healed.

"For I also am a man under authority. I have soldiers under me. I say to one man, 'Go', and he goes on my command. I say to another, 'Come', and he comes at my bidding. I order my servant to do something, and he does it."

The Centurion believed that just as he had authority from his commander to give orders and see them obeyed, so Jesus had power from God simply to say the word for a work of healing to be done.

When Jesus got this message, He was amazed, and turned to the people who were with Him. "I have not found great faith like this even from a Jew," He said.

When the messengers got back to the house, they found the servant who had been on the point of death quite recovered from his sickness. In all His other miracles, Jesus had touched or spoken to the person who was to be healed. But here He did not even see the sick man.

Luke tells us that Jesus did not even see the Roman Centurion either, but Matthew tells us that Jesus did see in that Roman soldier the first of many millions who, although they did not enjoy the privileges of the Children of Israel, would nevertheless become children of God, because they were willing to believe on His Son.

The Nobleman's Son

Here is another story of how Jesus healed a sick person without ever seeing him. This time it is the story of a boy, the son of a nobleman.

This nobleman, or high court official, lived in Capernaum. He was a very important person in the district and very rich. But all his power and wealth were of no use when his son became very ill. When he heard that Jesus was somewhere in Galilee, he set out on his horse to find Him, and at last found Him in Cana which was about twenty or thirty miles away. We shall hear more about this little village of Cana later on.

When the nobleman reached Cana, he found Jesus surrounded as usual by a great crowd of people. These were Galilæans who had seen Jesus do some wonderful things in Jerusalem, and were hoping He would do more. How they gaped when they saw the nobleman come riding up, his horse all lathered and dust-stained with the long, furious journey!

Looking at him, but speaking more to the crowd, Jesus said very sadly, "Unless you see signs and wonders, you will not believe."

Jesus never did miracles just to make people believe He was the Son of God. He wanted people to believe in Him for His own sake. He did the miracles because He loved men and women, boys and girls, and was grieved when they were sick and sad. He was so disappointed when people only wanted to see the miracles He did, but did not obey the words He spoke to them.

That is why He said so sadly, "Unless you see signs and wonders, you will not believe."

But the nobleman simply said to Jesus, "Sir, please come down before my boy dies."

Jesus, seeing how very troubled the poor father was, said, "Go your way; your son will get better."

The nobleman believed the word of Jesus. He did not

209

try to persuade Jesus to come to Capernaum and see the boy for Himself. He mounted his horse again and hurried away back home, perfectly satisfied that it would be quite all right if Jesus said it would be.

As he was coming near his own house, some of his servants came down the road to meet him with the glad news: "Your son is alive and well!"

The nobleman asked them, "When did he begin to get well again?"

"About one o'clock," they replied. And the nobleman remembered it was about one o'clock when Jesus said to him, "Go your way; your son will get better."

We do not know if the nobleman ever saw Jesus again, but we do know, for John tells us, that from that day the nobleman, and his little boy, and all the people in his house believed that Jesus was the Son of God.

~~~~~~

"What Manner of Man is This?"

Jesus spent only three years or so teaching and healing people. Most of that time was spent on the shores of the Sea of Galilee.

Frequently Jesus and His disciples would have to cross the sea from one place to another. Many of the disciples, you will remember, were fishermen, and, therefore, knew all about boats and how to sail them.

One night, after a very busy day, Jesus said to His disciples, "Let us sail over to the other side."

Mark tells us it was the evening of the same day on which Jesus told the story of the Sower. The crowd was so great that Jesus had to sit in the prow of a boat, using it as a kind of pulpit or platform from which to speak to the people who were sitting on the sandy shore.

Perhaps it was on this very same boat that they crossed over to the other side of the great Lake. If so, then the pulpit became a bed, for Jesus was so tired with all the work of the day that He fell sound asleep on the cushion, or pillow, which the fishermen used as a seat or a couch.

The Sea of Galilee lies nearly six hundred feet below sea-level, in a deep bowl formed by the hills all round it. Sometimes the wind comes rushing through the valleys in the hills and lashes the sea into a great fury. Just like when you blow into a cup of tea or bowl of soup.

Well, that is just what happened on this night of all nights. When the little boat was well into the Lake, a tornado hit the water with such force that even the experienced sailors among the disciples were panic-stricken. And all the time, Jesus was fast asleep!

The waves beat into the little ship until it looked as if it would sink, and then the terrified disciples went to Jesus to wake him up. "Master," they shouted at Him through the storm. "Master, don't you care if we perish?"

Jesus rose up and rebuked the wind, and said to the sea, "Peace, be still!" And the wind ceased, and there was a great calm.

"Why were you so afraid?" Jesus asked His disciples. "How is it that you have no faith?"

But now they were afraid with a different kind of fear. "What manner of man is this," they exclaimed to one another, "that even the wind and sea obey Him?"

This was indeed a wonderful miracle, but even more wonderful still is the way in which a countless number of the followers of Christ have recalled His words in times of great danger, "Peace, be still!"

Thousands upon thousands of them when faced with persecution, and even death, have remembered that Christ's presence was with them, and they have felt strangely safe and at peace.

Jesus Walks on the Sea

This is another story of a ship caught in a storm with the disciples in it. But this time, Jesus is not with them. It was the evening of that great day when, with the help of a little boy and his picnic-lunch, Jesus had fed over five thousand people.

After it was all over, Jesus told His disciples to get into a boat and go on before Him to the other side of the Lake of Galilee, while He sent the great crowd of people away to their homes. By the time this was done, it had become dark, and Jesus, instead of going to sleep, went on to the hillside alone to pray.

Jesus often did that after a busy day. He loved to pray to His Heavenly Father, and drew more strength and refreshment that way than He did from sleep. He prayed for a long time—till about three o'clock in the morning, but He had not forgotten His disciples.

Meantime, they were having a bad time. A strong, contrary wind was throwing up huge waves, and although they kept on toiling and rowing as hard as ever they could, they made no progress. Suddenly, in the half-light of the morning, they saw someone coming towards them walking on the water, and they were frightened. "It's a ghost!" they cried out in their fear.

But a well-loved voice came over the waters to them. "Be of good cheer! It is I! Be not afraid." It was Jesus. He had seen their distress and was coming to help them.

Peter called out, "Lord, if it is really You, bid me come to You on the water." And Jesus said to him, "Come!"

Peter got out of the ship and started to walk on the water to Jesus. But when he saw the boisterous waves, he lost his nerve, and began to sink. "Lord, save me!" he cried out.

Immediately, Jesus stretched out His hand and caught Peter. "O Peter," He said to him, "you are only half a believer. Why did you begin to doubt?"

Jesus and Peter then got into the ship, and the wind ceased.

All who were in the boat worshipped Jesus and said to Him, "Without doubt, You are the Son of God."

Now, these wonderful stories of Jesus are not just interest-

Jesus calms the wind and the sea.

ing stories. They are also intended to teach us very important lessons. There are two valuable lessons in this story.

First, although the disciples thought they were in the storm all alone, Jesus had not forgotten them. When they had come to the most difficult part of their way, He came to their help.

213

Secondly, Peter began to sink because he took his eyes off Jesus. It was when he saw the huge waves that he lost his nerve. If he had kept looking up and not down, he would have been quite safe.

There is a great text in the Bible, in the Epistle to the Hebrews. It comes right after the wonderful eleventh chapter in which we are given that long list of the heroes and heroines of our faith. Here is the text: "Seeing we are surrounded by so great a crowd of witnesses, let us throw away every weight, and especially the sin of unbelief which so easily besets us, and let us run with patience the race that is set before us, looking all the time to Jesus Who is our Captain and our Guide."

~~~~~~

"Launch Out into the Deep"

The four Evangelists—Matthew, Mark, Luke, and John— together give a complete picture of Jesus, but they each tell the story in his own way. This is how Luke describes the call of the three foremost disciples of Jesus—Peter, James, and John.

One day Jesus was walking by the Lake of Galilee not far from the city of Capernaum, when He came across two boats standing side by side. They belonged to two pairs of brothers who were partners in a firm of fishermen.

The boats were drawn up on to the beach, and the fishermen were cleaning and repairing their nets.

Jesus went on board one of the boats which happened to be Peter's, and He asked Peter if he would thrust his boat out into the sea a little from the shore.

Peter did so, and then Jesus from the ship taught the crowd that had gathered on the shore. We have seen that Jesus did this more than once.

When He had finished teaching the people, Jesus said to

214

Peter, "Take your boat out into the deep water, and let down your nets for a draught (or haul) of fish."

Peter, whose full name was Simon Peter, replied, "Master we have toiled all the night long, and have taken nothing. Nevertheless, because You tell us to do it, we will let down the net."

Hauling in the net full of fish.

So they rowed out into the deeper water, away from the shallows, and let down the net. When they pulled the net in again, it was so heavy and full of fish that it started to break, and they had to call to their partners in the other ship to come and help them. Both ships were soon full and in danger of sinking owing to the weight of the fish.

215

When Peter saw this marvellous catch of fish, he was so astonished that he fell on his knees and said, "Depart from me, for I am a sinful man, O Lord."

Peter realized that there was purity and power about Jesus that made him feel poor and mean. But Jesus did not leave him. He was never to leave Peter again, although Peter was to deny Him.

Jesus said to Peter, James, and John; and to Andrew, too, as we know from Matthew and Mark. "Fear not, from henceforth you will be fishers of men." When they brought their ships to land, they forsook everything and followed Him.

In this very telling way, Jesus was teaching those four men the great lesson of true discipleship. The men and women who have done most for the kingdom of God are not those who stood in the shallows on the shore afraid to launch out, but those who ventured out into the deep places, risking everything at the word of Jesus.

The Wedding at Cana

Cana, you remember, was the little place to which the nobleman came looking for Jesus to ask him to heal his sick son. At Cana there must have lived some family friends of Jesus, for Mary, the mother of Jesus, Jesus Himself, and some of His disciples had been invited to a marriage feast there.

A marriage feast in the East sometimes lasts for a whole week, and guests keep coming to it all the time. When Jesus arrived, Mary said to Jesus: "They have no wine."

In our Bible the reply Jesus gave to Mary sounds sharp, and almost rude. But we know Jesus could never have been rude to anyone, and least of all to His mother. This is a case where the English Bible fails to convey the real meaning. What Jesus really said was something like this, "Lady Mother, don't let it upset you. I must wait for the right moment."

So Mary said to the servants, "Just carry out the instructions He gives you."

Now, in or about the house were standing six large stone water-jars which nearly all Jews kept for certain religious services of purification.

Jesus said to the servants, "Fill the jars with water." And when they had done this, "Now draw out and take it to the steward of the feast."

When the steward, or, as we should call him, the Master of Ceremonies, tasted the water the servants brought to him, he thought it was the finest wine he had ever tasted.

He was so astonished that he went over to the bridegroom and said to him, "It is usually the custom to set out the best wine at the beginning of a feast, and the not-so-good towards the end, but you have kept the good wine until now."

The bridegroom did not know what the steward was talking about, nor did anyone else then, for only the servants knew that while what they put into the jars was clear water, what they drew out was wine.

Why did Jesus do this wonderful miracle? I think it was because He knew how terribly shamed and disgraced the bride and bridegroom would feel if the wine ran out before their wedding feast was over.

Perhaps Jesus knew that because He and His disciples had come towards the end of the feast, they had put a strain on the preparations that had been made, and He did not want the happy day to be spoilt for the young couple.

Whether this was the reason or not, it would have been just like the Saviour to be so thoughtful about others. It is lovely to think that He was present at the marriage feast to share in the happiness.

The next time you are present at a marriage service, listen for those words which the minister will say right at the beginning of the service, "Marriage is a holy estate Christ adorned and beautified with His presence, and the first miracle that He wrought, in Cana of Galilee."

It is lovely to know that Jesus will still grace with His presence every marriage service to which He is invited.

Jesus Brings Lazarus Back to Life

Only two men in the Bible have the name of Lazarus. One was the poor beggar in the parable who lay at the door of Dives the rich man. The other Lazarus was the only brother of Martha and Mary, whose home in Bethany Jesus loved so much to visit.

A great sorrow had come to this lovely little home. Lazarus had been taken suddenly and seriously ill. And Jesus, their great Friend, was not there to help them.

The rulers of the Jews, in the nearby city of Jerusalem, had decided to arrest Jesus, for they said Jesus was upsetting the people by His new teaching. And Jesus with His disciples had withdrawn, for the time being, beyond their reach.

Martha and Mary, however, knew where Jesus was, and they sent Him a message. It said very simply, "Lord, he whom You love so much is very ill."

When Jesus received the message, although He loved Martha and Mary and Lazarus very, very much, He stayed two days more, and then He said to His disciples, "Let us go back again into Judæa."

His disciples were dismayed to hear this. "Master," they said, "the Jews only the other day tried to stone You, and yet You want to go back there again!"

Jesus replied, "Our friend Lazarus is sleeping, and I go to awake him out of his sleep."

"But if he is sleeping, it will be good for him," the disciples replied. For they did not understand that Jesus really meant that Lazarus was already dead.

So Jesus had to tell them quite plainly that Lazarus was dead. "And I am glad for your sakes that I was not there," He said, "so that you may believe. But now let us go."

When the disciples saw that Jesus was determined to go to the place where His enemies were waiting for Him, one of them, whose name was Thomas, said to the others, "Let us also go that we may die with Him."

These were brave words, and no doubt Thomas meant them.

218

So did Peter and the others, but before very long, when the enemies of Jesus came to arrest Him, they all forsook Him and fled, and Peter even denied he had ever known Jesus.

When Martha heard that Jesus was coming, she went out to meet Him, but Mary sat in the house. "Lord," said Martha to Jesus, "if You had been here, my brother would not have died. But I know that even now whatever You ask from God, God will give it You."

"Your brother will rise again," Jesus said to her.

"Yes, I know," Martha replied. "He will rise again in the resurrection at the last day."

Jesus said, "I am the Resurrection, and the Life: he that believes in Me, though he dies, yet will he live again. And whoever lives and believes in Me will never die. Do you believe this, Martha?"

"Yes, Lord," replied Martha. "I believe You are the Christ, the Son of God, Who was to come into the world."

Martha then returned to the house to find Mary. She whispered to her, "The Master is come, and is asking for you." Mary sprang up and hurried to Jesus, and a number of her Jewish friends followed her, thinking she was going to the grave.

When Mary came to Jesus, she fell down at His feet, and said, "Lord, if You had been here, my brother would not have died." And she wept so bitterly that all her friends wept too.

Jesus was very upset when He saw how heart-broken they were, and He said, "Where have you laid Lazarus?"

When He saw the grave of Lazarus, the Bible says very simply, "Jesus wept".

"See how He loved Lazarus," they all said. But it was not only because He loved Lazarus that Jesus was weeping. It was also because He could see, as no one else could see, all the sorrow and suffering that sin had brought into the world.

The tomb of Lazarus was really a cave with a large stone in front of it. "Roll away the stone," Jesus commanded.

"But, Lord, Lazarus has been dead for four days!" exclaimed Martha.

"Did I not tell you, Martha," Jesus said gently to her, "that if you could only believe, you would see the wonder-working power of God?"

So they took away the stone. And Jesus looked up to Heaven and said, "Father, I thank You that You have heard my prayer."

Then with a loud voice He called, as if giving a command, "Lazarus, come out to Me!" And, to the wonder of all who were there, Lazarus came out of the tomb, still bound in his grave-clothes.

"Loose him, and let him go," said Jesus.

Many of the people who saw this wonderful miracle praised God for restoring Lazarus, and believed that Jesus was the Son of God. But some rushed off to report what had taken place to the Jewish rulers in Jerusalem.

The Jewish authorities were alarmed. "What are we going to do?" they said to one another. "This Man is doing many miracles. If we let Him go on, everybody will want to follow Him, and the Romans will say it is a rebellion. They will come and crush us, and we shall lose our position and power."

From that time, they plotted how they might best get rid of Jesus. And again Jesus withdrew with His disciples beyond the reach of His enemies.

So the chief priests in Jerusalem made an order that if any person knew where Jesus was he should report it to the authorities. They also offered a reward of thirty pieces of silver.

Because He had been so kind to so many people, and had shown to them a new and better way of knowing and serving God, Jesus brought upon Himself the anger of those who felt He was threatening their position and power.

And those kind hands that did such good,
They nailed them to a cross of wood.

Jesus is greeted by cheering crowds as He enters Jerusalem.

The First Palm Sunday

The little company was on its way to Jerusalem. Jesus walked alone ahead of His disciples. There was something about the set of His face and the firmness in His step that amazed them. They knew that something very serious was closing in on them. But they could not tell what; and they were very afraid.

Suddenly, Jesus turned to them. "Listen!" He said, "We are going up to Jerusalem; and the Son of Man will be betrayed into the hands of the rulers there, and they will condemn Him to death, and hand Him over to the Romans. And the Romans will mock Him, and scourge Him, and will spit upon Him, and will kill Him; and the third day He will rise again."

Jesus then turned again, and led His amazed and troubled disciples on the way to the great city.

It was the time of the great Feast of the Passover when hundreds of thousands of Jews from all over the world went up to Jerusalem. Knowing that the rulers wished to seize Jesus, many people wondered whether He would dare to show Himself in the city. "Do you think He will come to the Feast?" they asked one another.

The manner in which that question was answered has been specially remembered every year since, on the day we now call Palm Sunday.

Jesus had got as far as the little village of Bethany when He told two of His disciples to go on ahead. "Go your way," He directed them, " to the village in front of you, and just as you enter it, you will see a young colt tied on which no man has ever yet sat. Loose him, and bring him to Me.

"If any man," Jesus continued, "should say to you, 'Why are you doing this?' you are to reply, 'The Lord hath need of him', and he will at once let you have the colt."

And that is what happened. We do not know who the owner of the colt was, but he must have been one of the many who followed Jesus. When they brought the little animal to where Jesus was, the disciples put their coloured garments on the colt, and Jesus rode on it towards the city.

When others heard that Jesus was coming, some spread their garments on the road, as was sometimes done for a King, while others cut down palm branches from the trees, and waved them, shouting, "Hosanna! Hosanna! Blessed is He that comes in the name of the Lord: Hosanna in the highest!"

As Jesus rode through the city gates, the whole city was stirred. "Who is this?" many asked. And others replied, "This is Jesus, the prophet of Nazareth of Galilee."

But there was a deeper meaning to it than that. Matthew tells us, in his Gospel, that all this was done to remind the people of the Old Testament prophecy in the book of Zechariah: "Rejoice greatly, O daughter of Zion; shout O daughter of Jerusalem. Look! your King comes to you. He is a just King and victorious; but He comes lowly, and riding upon an ass, and upon a colt the foal of an ass."

Jesus was trying to show that great crowd of people the kind of King He was, and the kind of Kingdom He had come to set up. He had not come as a mighty warrior-king, with sword and armour, riding on a war-horse. He had come

222

meek and lowly, riding on the patient little animal that speaks of peace and quietness.

Jesus is not a conqueror like Alexander, or Napoleon, or Hitler. He does not compel the allegiance of men by force, but wins their loyalty by love.

~~~~~~

The Christian Passover

We have seen how the Jewish Passover was instituted on the night when each Jewish family sprinkled the blood of a little lamb on the doorposts of their houses. We have also seen how every year since that night the Angel of Death " passed over " them, the Jews have observed the great Passover Feast.

During the week that followed the first Palm Sunday, the Passover Feast was due to be held, and Jesus with His disciples planned to observe it too.

" Where would you like us to prepare for You to eat the Passover? " His disciples asked Him.

In reply, Jesus said to two of His disciples, " Go ye into the city, and there you will meet a man carrying a pitcher of water. Follow him and when you see him enter a house, say to the owner of that house, ' Where is the guest-chamber where the Master may eat the Passover with His disciples? ' And he will show you a large upper room already furnished and prepared. There make ready for us."

The two disciples carried out their instructions, and made ready for the Passover, and in the evening Jesus came with His disciples.

As they were eating the Passover, Jesus suddenly said, " I tell you of a truth that one of you will betray Me."

They all became very sad when they heard this terrible news, and each said to Him, " Lord, surely it cannot be me? "

" It is one of the twelve who is sharing in the same dish with Me," Jesus answered. The disciples did not understand then what He meant.

Towards the end of the meal, Jesus picked up a loaf of bread, gave thanks, and broke it into pieces, and gave each disciple a share. "Take, eat," He said; "this is My body, which is given for you: this do in remembrance of Me."

He then took a cup of wine, and when He had again given thanks to God, He passed the cup round, saying, "This is My blood which is shed for many."

Jesus passes the cup of wine to His disciples.

Ever since that night, the Christian Church has observed, not the Jewish Passover, but what has come to be known as the Sacrament of the Last Supper, and not just once a year but many times.

The Sacrament of the Last Supper, or the Holy Communion, has a double purpose. First, it is a memorial feast. It is in remembrance of Christ's death upon the Cross when His body was broken and His blood shed for us.

Secondly, it has an even deeper meaning. Bread and wine

224

were the simple, everyday food of the people by which they fed themselves and nourished their bodies to keep them well and strong for their daily toil and service. They could not live without this food.

So when, at the Last Supper, Jesus gave His disciples bread and wine, calling these His flesh and blood, it was to show His people that, just as they could not live their ordinary lives without bread and wine, neither could they live Christian lives without Him. In a very real sense He must be their daily food.

Jesus is Betrayed

It is one of the great, sad mysteries of history that Jesus was betrayed to His enemies by one of His own disciples. We shall never know why.

Judas Iscariot was one of the twelve who were nearest to Jesus. For nearly three years he had been in the company of Jesus, watching all the wonderful things He did, and hearing all the wonderful words He said. And yet at the last he betrayed Jesus to His enemies.

He went to the chief priests and said to them, "What will you give me to deliver Him into your hands?" They agreed to give him thirty pieces of silver. And from that time Judas looked for the best moment to betray Jesus. It all had to be done as secretly as possible, for the authorities did not want any trouble with the people; they were not sure how many of the people really followed Jesus.

Even after Judas had agreed with the chief priests to betray Him, he went with the others to eat the Passover with Jesus.

In the East, it is the custom for all present at a meal sometimes to eat from the same dish. If the host wishes specially to honour any of the guests, he will take a piece of bread

225

and dip it into the dish and then hand it to the guest as a particularly tasty morsel.

During the Supper, Jesus took a piece of bread, dipped it into the dish, and gave it to Judas. It was an act of friendship. Jesus was making a last appeal to Judas to remain loyal to Him.

Their eyes must have met when Jesus handed Judas the morsel, and Jesus saw that Judas had gone too far to draw back, so He said to him, " What you have decided to do, do quickly."

Judas went out, " and it was night ", the Bible says. It was, indeed, a dark night for Judas, although the moon would be shining bright and full at the time of the Passover.

The other disciples did not seem to notice that anything unusual had taken place. They thought that Jesus had sent Judas out on a special errand—perhaps to give something to the poor, as was the custom at the time of the Passover.

After Judas had gone, Jesus spoke to His other disciples some of the loveliest words in all the Gospels. For example, when they began to feel that something very sad was going to happen, although they did not know then what it was, Jesus comforted them by telling them of the heavenly mansions.

" Let not your heart be troubled," He said; " you believe in God, believe also in Me. In My Father's house are many mansions (or places): if it were not so, I would have told you. I go to prepare a place for you. And if I go and prepare a place for you, I will come again, and receive you to Myself; that where I am, there you may be also."

When Jesus had finished speaking, they all sang a Passover psalm together, then went out into the Mount of Olives.

*   *   *   *

Below the Mount of Olives there is an olive garden called Gethsemane. Many thousands of people visit it every year for Jesus loved to go there to pray, and it was there that He was finally betrayed and arrested.

When Jesus and His eleven disciples entered the garden, after they had left the upper room where they had shared the Last Supper together, He told eight of them to wait near the gate. "Sit ye here, while I pray," He said to them.

Taking Peter, James, and John, He went on a little distance into the garden, and then asked them also to wait. "Wait here and watch," He told them.

Jesus then went forward a little farther alone, and fell on the ground and prayed, "Father, all things are possible to You; take away this cup from me: nevertheless not what I will, but what You will."

We can never know what Jesus meant by "this cup". It was something so terrible to think about that, as He prayed, "*His sweat was as it were great drops of blood falling down to the ground.*"

But when Jesus prayed, "Nevertheless, not what I will, but what You will," great peace came to Him, and He was ready and willing to do what God had sent Him into the world to do.

When Jesus returned to His disciples, He found them asleep. "Why sleep ye?" He said to them. "Rise and pray, lest you fall into temptation."

Just then a great crowd of people and soldiers came into the garden, all armed with swords and clubs. They were from the chief priests, and at their head was Judas who knew that Jesus would be in the garden at this time.

Judas had warned his accomplices beforehand that he would go up and kiss the one they were to arrest. This was the usual way for a disciple to greet his Master, and Judas used this as the signal for the soldiers to pick out Jesus in the darkness.

As he had arranged, Judas went up to Jesus. "Hail, Master!" he said, and kissed Him.

"Judas," said Jesus, "do you betray the Son of Man with a kiss?"

Jesus then turned to the soldiers and said to them, "Whom do you seek?" They replied, "Jesus of Nazareth."

"I am He," said Jesus, and as He said that they all fell back.

Peter had brought a sword with him, and he struck at the soldiers, and hurt the ear of a man called Malchus. Jesus

227

said to Peter, "Put up your sword, Peter, into its sheath; the cup which my Father has given Me, will I not drink it?" and He healed the ear of Malchus, who was a servant of the high priest.

"Why do you come to Me as against a thief, with swords and clubs?" He said to the chief priests. "When I was daily with you in the Temple, you did not put your hands on Me. But this is your hour, and the power of darkness."

When the disciples saw that their Leader was offering no resistance, but submitting Himself to His enemies, they scattered and fled into the surrounding darkness. Then the soldiers bound Jesus, and led Him away to the palace of the high priest.

~~~~~~

The Trial of Jesus

Caiaphas, the high priest of that time, was a crafty old man. He had already made up his mind that the sooner Jesus was out of the way the better it would be for him and all who like him were afraid that they would lose their positions and privileges if Jesus lived.

Although it was midnight when Jesus was brought to his house, he summoned the chief priests and rulers to come and put Jesus on trial.

It was like many of the trials we hear of to-day that take place in some other countries—the witnesses were told what to say beforehand, and the sentence was fixed before the trial began.

That sentence was death. But the Jewish authorities did not have the power to put anyone to death, so Jesus was taken to the house of Pontius Pilate, the Roman Governor of Palestine.

Pilate said to the chief priests, "What accusation do you bring against this Man?"

228

In the Garden of Gethsemane.

"If our accusation had not been a serious one, we would not have brought Him to you," was the impertinent reply.

"Take Him and judge Him according to your own law," retorted Pilate.

"It is not lawful for us to put any man to death," came the quick reply, and Pilate realized that this was indeed a serious matter.

Then the chief priests began to accuse Jesus before Pilate. "We found this fellow," they said, "perverting the nation. He was urging the people not to pay tribute to Caesar, declaring that He Himself was Christ, the King of Israel."

So long as the chief priests repeated their accusations before Pilate, Jesus never answered a word. Pilate said to Him, "Do you not hear how many things they witness against You?"

But still Jesus kept silent, and Pilate wondered greatly at Him. He knew quite well that the chief priests were not speaking the truth, but that it was for envy they had delivered Jesus to him. So he examined Jesus in private.

"Are You really the King of the Jews?" he asked Jesus.

"Do you think so yourself?" Jesus replied. "Or did others tell you?"

"Am I a Jew?" the proud Roman answered back. "Your own people have delivered You to me. What have you done?"

"My Kingdom is not an earthly kingdom," Jesus replied. "If it were, then would my followers fight that I should not be delivered to the Jews: But My Kingdom will not come in that way."

"Are You then some kind of King?" asked Pilate.

"Yes," Jesus replied. "It was for this that I came into the world, that the Kingdom of truth should be established. Everyone that is for the truth will recognize that I am the Truth."

"What is truth?" said Pilate. The Romans knew there were many kinds of religions, and when Pilate asked "What is truth?" he meant that, as far as he was concerned, one was as good as another. He did not wait for an answer,

"Crucify Him! Crucify Him!"

or what followed might have taken a very different turn.

While Pilate was examining Jesus in this way he received a note from his wife. *"Have nothing to do with that just Man,"* Pilate read, *"for I have suffered many things this day in a dream because of Him."*

Pilate's wife had probably heard a lot about Jesus. Pilate had spies out in the streets, and perhaps they had told her about the teaching of Jesus, and of the wonderful miracles

231

He had done. She must have thought so much about Jesus, that she actually dreamt about Him.

She realized that there was something about Jesus that was different from all other religious teachers, and she was afraid her husband would be committing a great wrong if he harmed Jesus in any way.

So Pilate decided to save Jesus. He went to the chief priests who were waiting outside, and said to them, " I find no fault in Him at all.

" We have a custom," he continued, " that I should release a prisoner to you at the time of the Passover. Would you not like me to release this man who calls Himself the King of the Jews? "

But the chief priests started shouting, " No, not this man. Release unto us Barabbas." Barabbas was a man who had led a rebellion against the Romans, and was therefore a popular person with the Jews.

When that plan failed, Pilate tried another. He ordered Jesus to be scourged. That was a cruel form of punishment. The soldiers lashed Jesus with whips tipped with pieces of iron.

One soldier made a crown of thorns and pressed it on the head of Jesus. Then he got an old purple robe and put it on Jesus, and put a reed in His hand. All the other soldiers then saw what the brutal joke meant, and they bowed down before Jesus, " Hail, King of the Jews! " they mocked at Him.

Then Pilate took Jesus as He was, still wearing the crown of thorns and the purple robe, out to the great crowd of people. " Behold, the man! " he cried to them. " I bring Him out to you, that you may know I find no fault in Him."

Perhaps, he thought that when they saw Jesus, after He had suffered the scourging and the mocking, the people would take pity on Him and let Him go. If so, he was again disappointed, for the chief priests and the others shouted, " Crucify Him! Crucify Him! "

" Take you Him yourself and crucify Him," retorted Pilate, " for I find no fault in Him."

" We have a law, and by our law He ought to die, because

He made Himself the Son of God," the chief priests said. They were determined that Pilate should pass the sentence.

Pilate again took Jesus aside, and he said to Him, " Who are You, and where *do* You come from? "

This time Jesus kept silent before Pilate. He realized that Pilate was more afraid of the people than he was of doing a wicked thing. So He did not answer.

" So You will not speak? " said Pilate. " Don't you know I have the power to crucify You or to release You? "

" You could have no power at all against Me," said Jesus, " except it were given you from above."

Then Pilate again tried hard to release Jesus, but the Jews cried out, " If you let this man go, you are no friend of Caesar's. For anyone who makes himself to be a King is against Caesar."

That was enough! If Pilate feared any man it was Caesar. He knew those Jews were quite capable of sending false reports to Caesar in Rome. So he tried one more move to shift the responsibility.

He sent for a basin of water and washed his hands before all the people. " I am clear of the blood of this innocent person," he declared. " See you to it."

And he delivered Jesus to them, and released Barabbas.

The First Good Friday

Death by crucifixion was one of the most cruel and shameful forms of punishment ever invented. It was devised by the Romans to punish criminals and runaway slaves.

The person to be crucified was nailed by the hands and feet to a cross made of two beams of wood. The cross was then lifted up, and the victim left hanging there to die a slow and agonizing death. The victim, too, had to carry his cross to the place of execution.

When Jesus had been condemned, they laid the heavy cross on His shoulders and led Him away to a place called Calvary, outside the city wall.

After all the trial and scourging and mocking that Jesus had gone through, He fainted under the heavy weight of the cross, so they took it from Him, and compelled a man, one of the crowd, to carry it. This man's name was Simon. This Simon was from Cyrene, in North Africa, and had probably come to Jerusalem for the Passover. An ancient story says he was a black man, but we cannot be sure of that.

We do not know what Simon thought when he was picked out from the crowd to carry the cross of Jesus. But we do know that his two sons, Alexander and Rufus, became Christians. So we would not be far wrong if we thought that when the cross was shifted from the shoulders of Jesus to those of Simon, Jesus spoke to him and thanked him, and that what Jesus said to him made Simon become a Christian too.

There were two others in that grim procession carrying crosses. They were two thieves who were to be crucified along with Jesus. When they came to Calvary, the three crosses were erected on the top of the hill, and the cross of Jesus was in the middle.

A great crowd of people had come to watch the sad scene, amongst them the chief priests and rulers. As Jesus looked down upon them from His cross, He prayed, "Father, forgive them for they know not what they do."

But they jeered back at Him. "He saved others; let Him save himself, if He is the Christ, the chosen of God."

And the soldiers also mocked Him again, offering Him sour wine to drink, and saying to Him. "If you are the King of the Jews, save Yourself."

Over His head, on which perhaps the crown of thorns still rested, they nailed an inscription, written in the three languages used in Palestine—Hebrew, Greek, and Latin—"THIS IS THE KING OF THE JEWS".

They had stripped off His clothes, and at the foot of the Cross the soldiers gambled with dice to pick out who should win the seamless robe of Jesus; that same robe which the woman touched and was healed—the woman who had spent all her money on doctors and medicines before she met Jesus.

On either side of Jesus hung one of the thieves. One shouted and swore at Him, "If You are the Christ, save Yourself and us too."

The other thief rebuked his companion, "Do you not fear God," he said, "seeing you are getting the same treatment

The first Good Friday.

as He is? And it is just enough as far as we are concerned, for we deserve what we are getting. But this man has done nothing to deserve it."

Then this thief turned his head to Jesus and said to Him, "Lord, remember me, when You come into Your kingdom."

And Jesus said to the penitent thief, "Of a truth, I say to you, to-day you will be with Me in Paradise."

Suddenly, an eclipse came over the sun, and for three hours there was a great darkness, although it was still the middle of the day.

Then Jesus called out in a loud voice, "It is finished! Father, into Thy hands I commend My spirit." And with that He died.

The Centurion who was in charge of the soldiers, and who had watched how Jesus had suffered so patiently, and had died forgiving His enemies, exclaimed with reverence, "This was indeed a righteous man."

The great crowd who had come to see this spectacle returned to Jerusalem, and many smote their breasts with grief and anguish because of all they had seen.

So ended the first Good Friday. Perhaps you are wondering what was good about a day like this when Jesus, Who was so kind and loving, had to suffer so much on the cruel cross.

Do you remember these verses from the hymn "There is a green hill far away"? We may find part of the answer there.

> *We may not know, we cannot tell*
> *What pains He had to bear.*
> *But we believe it was for us*
> *He hung and suffered there.*
>
> *He died that we might be forgiven,*
> *He died to make us good,*
> *That we might go at last to heaven*
> *Saved by His precious blood.*

The First Easter

It is a strange thing that when Jesus was arrested everybody forsook Him and fled, yet after He died on the Cross many began to declare quite publicly their loyalty to Him.

Amongst them were two very important men. One was

called Nicodemus. He was the Nicodemus who had once called to see Jesus during the night, because he was afraid to do it during the day.

The other was Joseph, a wealthy man from the town of Arimathaea. Joseph was important and wealthy enough to go to Pilate and beg that the body of Jesus should be given into his care.

Pilate could not believe at first that Jesus had died so quickly and he asked the Centurion about it. When the Centurion reported that Jesus was really dead, Pilate gave Joseph permission to take the body.

Joseph had some time before prepared a tomb for himself in a garden near the place where Jesus had been crucified. It had never yet been used, and, with the help of Nicodemus, Joseph laid the body of Jesus in the new tomb.

Nicodemus had brought with him a large and costly mixture of aloes and myrrh, and together they anointed the body of Jesus and wrapped it in new linen cloths, as was the custom of that day.

The tomb was really a cave dug into the side of a rock, and a huge, heavy stone was rolled into the mouth of the cave to close it up, so as to prevent robbers or wild animals from getting into it.

The chief priests went to Pilate and said to him, "Sir, we remember that while this deceiver was still alive, He said that after three days He would rise again.

"We request you," they went on, "to give an order that the sepulchre where they have buried Him be made sure, lest His disciples come by night, and steal His body away, and then say to the people that He is risen from the dead. If that were to happen the last error would be worse than the first."

Pilate said to them, "You have your own Temple guard. Go and make it as safe as you can."

So they went, and made the grave quite safe, putting a huge seal on the stone, so that if it were moved the seal would be broken. To make doubly sure, they left a soldier on guard over it.

It was Friday when the body of Jesus was taken down from the cross and placed in the tomb. The next day, being the seventh day of the week, was the Jewish Sabbath, during which no work could be done.

The day following was the first day of the week, and this particular "first day" is the most famous of all days. For on this day took place the most wonderful happening in all history.

Early in the dawning of that first day, as soon as it began to be light, some of the women who had followed Jesus to the very end went to the sepulchre, or tomb.

They had taken with them sweet-smelling spices with which to anoint the body of Jesus. But they wondered how they would be able to do this. Who would roll away the heavy stone for them? As they got near to the sepulchre, to their great astonishment they saw that someone had rolled the stone away already.

When they crept nearer to the open tomb and were able to see inside, they saw that the body of Jesus was gone. But where Jesus had been lying they saw two angels in shining garments, one at the head and one at the foot.

The women were very afraid, and bowed themselves down to the ground. But the angels spoke kindly to them. "Why do you seek Him that is alive among the dead?" they asked. "He is not here. He is risen. Do you not remember how He said to you when He was still in Galilee that the Son of Man must be delivered into the hands of sinful men, and be crucified, and rise again on the third day?"

Then they remembered that Jesus had told them all these things; only they had not understood them then. But they did understand now, and they hurried away back to where they knew the apostles and disciples had gathered, to tell them the wonderful news.

The apostles and the others thought they were telling made-up stories, and did not believe them. But Peter and John ran off to the sepulchre to see for themselves what had really happened. John, being the younger of the two, outran Peter and got to the sepulchre first.

Stooping down, John looked into the sepulchre and saw the linen clothes, the head-napkin where the head of Jesus had been, and the other clothes lying as if He had slipped out of them without moving them at all. Then Peter came up and went in, and he, too, saw the clothes lying in that strange position; but he could not understand it.

John went right in then and looked at the clothes again, and realized that nobody could have unwrapped the clothes, but that the body of Jesus must have just come out of them by passing right through them. But even John did not then quite understand what this meant.

The two apostles returned home again. But Mary Magdalene remained behind, waiting and weeping at the sepulchre.

Suddenly she saw the two angels in white again. They said to her, "Woman, why are you weeping?" And Mary replied, "Because they have taken away my Lord, and I do not know where they have laid Him."

As she said that, she turned round to see who had come up behind her. In the misty morning light, she thought the figure was that of the gardener who looked after the garden.

She said to him, "Sir, if you have taken Him away, tell me where you have laid Him, and I will take Him away."

The figure said, "Mary!" When Mary heard that loved voice, she said, "Master!" and went to embrace His feet.

"Touch Me not," Jesus said to her, "for I am not yet ascended to My Father. But go to My brethren, and say to them, I am ascending to My Father and your Father; to My God and to your God."

And Mary ran to tell the glad news, "Christ is risen, indeed!"

That same evening, the disciples were gathered behind locked doors, because they were afraid of the Jews. Suddenly, Jesus stood amongst them, and said to them, "Peace be unto you."

As He said that, He showed them His hands that had been pierced by the nails, and the side that had been pierced by a Roman soldier to make sure He was really dead. How glad they were to see with their own eyes that their beloved Friend was no longer dead, but alive.

The apostle Thomas was not there when Jesus came that evening. The others said to him, "We have seen the Lord."

But Thomas, who ever since then has been nicknamed "Doubting Thomas", replied, "Except I can see in His hands the print of the nails, and put my finger into the print of the nails, and thrust my hand into His side, I will not believe."

Thomas meant that if the Person the others said they had seen was really Jesus, then He would bear on His body the marks of the wounds of the Cross.

Eight days later, the apostles and disciples were again gathered in the room, and this time Thomas was with them. Once more Jesus appeared in their midst, and said, "Peace be unto you." Then He said to Thomas, "Reach hither your finger, and feel My hands; and reach hither your hand, and put it into My side; and do not doubt, but believe."

Thomas did not venture to touch Jesus, but fell on his knees, saying, "My Lord and my God."

"Thomas," said Jesus to him, "because you have seen Me, you have believed: blessed are they that have not seen, and yet believe."

So ended this greatest of all days, and ever since then the first day of the week has been observed as the Christian Sabbath, or Sunday. It is also called the "Lord's Day", because on that day we specially remember that Jesus Who was crucified, rose from the dead, and is alive for evermore.

On the Way to Emmaus

Two of the disciples were on their way home to the little village of Emmaus which was a few hours journey on foot from Jerusalem. As they walked along the dusty road, they went over together all that they had seen and heard during

Peter and John go inside the empty tomb.

the past few days, and what they were talking about made them look very sad.

Just then another traveller joined their company, and went along with them. "What are you talking about that makes you look so sad?" the stranger asked them.

One of the two, whose name was Cleopas, replied, "Where have you been all this time that you do not seem to know the things which have happened recently in Jerusalem?"

"What things?" asked the stranger.

"The things concerning Jesus of Nazareth," they answered. "He was a prophet, mighty in deed and word before God and all the people. The chief priests and our rulers delivered Him to be condemned, and have crucified Him.

"We had hoped," they went on sadly, "that He was the One promised in the Scriptures Who should come to set our nation free.

"Yes, and what is more, although it is three days since all this happened, only this morning some of the women of our company amazed us with stories of how they had been to the sepulchre where He was buried, and found it empty. They also said they saw angels who said Jesus was alive.

"Some others of our company went to the sepulchre and found it empty, even as the women had said. But they did not see Jesus."

And that seemed to be the end, as far as they could see, and now they were on their way home, broken-hearted and with all their hopes dashed to the ground.

"Oh, you foolish ones, and slow to believe all that the prophets have said;" the stranger said to them, "can you not see that Christ had to suffer all these things before He could enter into His glory?"

Then he repeated to them Scripture after Scripture, beginning with the books of Moses and going through the various books of the prophets, to show to them that all that had happened in Jerusalem was but the fulfilment of the prophecies in the Old Testament.

By this time, they were coming into Emmaus, and the stranger made as if he intended to go farther on.

"Stay with us," they said to him, "for it is nearly evening, and the day is far spent." So he went into the house with them.

As they were having supper together, the stranger picked up a loaf of bread from the table. He blessed it, and brake it, and gave a piece of the bread to each of them.

They gazed at him in wonder. Where had they heard of this before? Yes, the apostles had told them how Jesus had blessed and broken the bread at the Last Supper.

And as they looked up again, He was gone! It had been Jesus all the time! Then they said to one another, "We might have known it! Did not our hearts burn within us while He talked to us by the way, and while He opened up to us the Scriptures?"

And without waiting another moment, they hurried back to Jerusalem to tell the others of all that had happened, and how they recognized Jesus when He broke the bread in their home.

Jesus Returns to Heaven

As a little baby born in Bethlehem, Jesus had come from Heaven. Now that the work He had been sent by His Father to do was finished, the time had come for Him to go back to His Father in Heaven.

It was forty days since the first Easter Sunday, and during that time the Lord Jesus had taught His disciples that they were now to carry on the work He had begun. And He promised them that although they would not be able to see Him, He would still be with them, guiding and helping them. "Go into all the world and preach the gospel to all nations," He told them, "and always remember I am with you, even to the end of the world."

Now they were meeting for the last time on the Bethany

243

hill where they had met so often before. Some of His disciples asked Him, "Are You now going to make Israel the great nation it once was in the days of old?"

Perhaps they thought that, since He had conquered death, the Lord Jesus would now conquer all who opposed the truth as well, and set up His glorious Kingdom in which there would be no evil or dark shadow.

But the Lord Jesus had to tell them that no one could say when the Kingdom would come. Only God Himself knew that. Meantime, there was much to be done: there was a whole world to be won. What had happened in these recent days was only the beginning of a great adventure that would demand all they had to give.

But they would not be able to do this in their own strength. Strength would be given them from above. The Spirit which had been upon Jesus would thenceforward also be upon them. All they would have to do would be to trust and obey. But first they must wait in Jerusalem for the signal from Heaven.

"The power of the Holy Spirit will come upon you," the Lord said to His little band of followers, "and then you will be My witnesses in Jerusalem, in Judaea, in Samaria, and even unto the uttermost part of the earth."

As He spoke, the Lord Jesus lifted up His pierced hands over them in blessing, and, as He blessed them, He slowly ascended up into the sky. A radiant cloud came between Him and them, and they saw Him no more.

As they stood gazing up into the now empty sky, the disciples suddenly realized that two angels in dazzling white stood by them. "Why do you stand gazing up into Heaven?" the angels asked them. "This same Jesus Who is taken from you like this into Heaven, will come as you have seen Him go."

With this glad assurance ringing in their hearts, the disciples returned to Jerusalem to wait there for the promised sign that the Great Adventure had begun.

The First Whitsuntide

Fifty days after the Passover, the Jews celebrated the Feast of Pentecost. It was a kind of harvest thanksgiving, when the first-fruits were presented in the Temple.

It was for them, as the harvest is for us, a time of gladness and gratitude for the good gifts of the earth. Almost as many Jews came up for this feast as for the Passover, especially from other countries to which so many Jews had emigrated.

Many of the followers of Jesus had gathered together with the apostles in one large room in Jerusalem. They had met to pray together and to hear from the apostles all the wonderful news about the Lord Jesus Who had died but was alive again, and of the things He had said before He had ascended to His Father in Heaven.

Suddenly, there was the sound as of a mighty wind rushing through the house where they were sitting, and they all saw a glowing light breaking up into little tongues of flame hovering over the head of each one there.

The effect on those people was tremendous. They were filled with a great power and ecstasy which compelled them to speak about the wonderful works of God in such a way that all the Jews from so many different parts of the world could understand what they were saying.

Some said, "What can this mean?" Others said, "These people are drunk with wine." But Peter, with the apostles and disciples standing around him, preached the first Christian sermon ever heard.

"These people are not drunk with wine, as ye suppose," he said to the people, who had come crowding round. "What has happened now is what the prophet Joel, in the Old Testament, said would happen. 'It shall come to pass, God has said, I will pour out of My Spirit upon all men: and your sons and daughters will be as holy prophets. Your young men will see visions, and your old men dream dreams: and on my servants, men and women alike, I will pour out My Spirit in those days.'"

This was the secret that Jesus had told His disciples would be made known after He had gone away. This was the promise of the Father for which they were to wait in Jerusalem, before going out to preach the Gospel to the uttermost ends of the earth. It was the signal that the Great Adventure had begun.

"Men of Israel," Peter went on, "listen to me. Jesus of Nazareth was sent by God. Only one sent by God could have done the good and great things which He did. Yet it was this Person sent by God that you seized, and by wicked hands crucified on a cross.

"Let this be known to all," he concluded, "that this same Jesus, Whom you crucified, God has raised from the dead and made to be the Saviour of the world."

When they heard this courageous message from Peter, many of the people were cut to the heart by the sense of their guilt, and they cried out to the apostles and disciples, "What shall we do?"

Then Peter said to them, "Confess your sin and sorrow, and be baptized every one of you in the name of Jesus Christ, so that you may have your sins forgiven, and you, too, will receive this gift of the Holy Spirit, as we have done. For this promise is for you as well as for us, and for your children, and, indeed, for everybody everywhere. For whosoever will call upon the name of the Lord will be saved."

Many of the great crowd gladly accepted Peter's word, and three thousand of them were baptized and became followers of the Lord Jesus.

In this wonderful way the Christian Church was born, and day by day it grew stronger and stronger, as more and more people heard the good news and believed it.

Every year since those wonderful events took place nearly 2,000 years ago, the Christian Church has observed three great Festivals. They are Christmas, when Jesus was born in Bethlehem; Easter, when He rose from the dead; and Whitsuntide, when He sent His Holy Spirit to be with those who love His Name and long to spread its fame amongst men.

The First Martyr

The Church grew so rapidly that soon the Apostles were quite unable to manage all the work. For in those days the followers of Jesus shared with one another all they possessed. And it was not easy to make sure that all had fair shares.

The Apostles called a meeting of all the disciples and said, "It is not sensible that we should leave off teaching and preaching the Word of God in order to look after matters of food and clothing, and so on. Choose from among yourselves seven men who are fully trusted among you, and who are wise and filled with the Holy Spirit. Let them look after all business matters, so that we may give all our time to prayer and teaching."

The disciples thought this was an excellent plan, and they chose seven men, of whom Stephen was the leader. Stephen was indeed filled with the Holy Spirit. In many ways he reminded men of Jesus Himself. So much was this the case that the religious leaders thought that they would have to get rid of Stephen, as they believed they had got rid of Jesus.

They arrested Stephen and dragged him before the High Council which was held in the Temple. They got witnesses to give a false impression of what Stephen had said to the people.

"This fellow will not stop saying wicked things against this holy place, and against our law," they declared.

"We have heard him say," they went on, "that this Jesus of Nazareth will destroy the Temple, and change the customs which Moses gave us."

All the council looked on Stephen, but they did not see one who showed fear of them. They saw his face shine like the face of an angel. Then the high priest said to Stephen, "Is it true what these witnesses say?"

In his reply, Stephen told the council the story of the Jewish people. How God had chosen Abraham and promised that in Abraham's children all the nations of the earth would be blessed.

247

Stephen reminded them how God had delivered their fathers from the land of Egypt, and had brought them through the wilderness to the Promised Land, with Moses as their leader. It was not because of anything they had done, but because of God's free love.

Saul looks on as Stephen is stoned.

He spoke of Joshua, and of David, and of Solomon and of the great Temple he built. And of the prophets which God had sent one after another to show them the way in which they should live in order to please God, and who had foretold the coming of the Saviour.

248

But they had seldom listened to the prophets. "You are a stubborn and sinful people," cried Stephen. "You always resist the Holy Spirit: as your fathers did, so do you."

"Which of the prophets have your fathers not persecuted?" Stephen asked the High Council. "*They* killed those who foretold the coming of the Just One. And *you* have now been the betrayers and murderers of that One."

When the Council heard this brave speech of Stephen's, they were cut to the heart, and hissed through their teeth at him. But Stephen gazed up into Heaven with a bright and happy smile. "Look!" he said, "I see the Heavens opened, and the Son of Man standing at the right hand of God."

When they heard this, they all rushed at him with a great shout of rage, and swept him off to a place outside the city walls. There they stoned him. As they stoned him, Stephen prayed to God, and said, "Lord Jesus, receive my spirit." And then he knelt down and cried so that all could hear him, "Lord, do not lay this sin to their charge." So Stephen died, as he had lived, in the Spirit of the Master he loved so well.

Those who stoned Stephen had first taken off their heavy cloaks, and laid them at the feet of a young man whose name was Saul. This young man Saul does not seem to have been one of those who stoned Stephen, but he approved of what the others were doing, and guarded their clothes. But as long as he lived, Saul never forgot the look of pure joy on the face of Stephen as he said, "Lord Jesus, receive my spirit!"

Stephen was the first of many, many martyrs who have died for the faith. Have you ever heard the saying, "*The blood of the martyrs is the seed of the Church*"? We shall now see how very true this is.

On the Damascus Road

Saul, the young man who guarded the clothes of those who stoned Stephen, was born in Tarsus, a famous city in the district we now know as Anatolia in Turkey. His father had been one of the many Jews who had gone abroad to set up business for themselves in foreign lands. A strict Pharisee himself, he wished his son to become a Rabbi, or teacher of the Jewish law. While he was still a boy, Saul was sent all the way to Jerusalem to be taught by a famous teacher called Gamaliel.

Saul grew up to be a very earnest and patriotic Jew, and a master of the Jewish scriptures and laws. He hated this new religion of Jesus of Nazareth, and resolved to stamp it out, and he soon became the leader of the enemies of the young Church.

He received the authority of the high priest to arrest the Christians wherever he could find them and to put them in prison, there to await death, if they did not deny the Lord Jesus. The name of Saul became a word that brought fear into the hearts of many men and women, and children too.

One day he was on his way to the city of Damascus to arrest some of the Christians there. With him was a company of soldiers. As they rode along the road, suddenly a light shone from heaven brighter than the noon-day sun, and Saul fell to the ground. He heard a Voice from Heaven say to him, " Saul, Saul, why do you persecute Me? "

" Who are you, Lord? " said the amazed Saul, with his face in the dust of the Damascus road.

" I am Jesus, Whom you are persecuting: it is hard for you to kick against the goad," replied the Voice from Heaven.

From this we may learn that the Holy Spirit had been pricking the conscience of Saul. The sight of Stephen's face, which Saul could never forget, was one of those pricks. But Saul had been kicking against them like some stubborn ox, and refusing to see the truth.

But now he could no longer escape the truth. The despised

Christians were right. Jesus of Nazareth was indeed the Son of God. The One Who had died on the Cross had indeed risen from the dead, and was now speaking to him from Heaven. In great fear and trembling, Saul said, "What do you wish me to do, Lord?"

Saul is suddenly blinded by a bright light.

"Go into the city, and you will be told there what you must do," was the reply.

The men who were with Saul had not heard the Voice. When the bright light had passed, they lifted Saul up, and found he was blind. They took him by the hand, and led him into the city of Damascus.

In the city of Damascus there lived a Christian disciple

251

called Ananias. He was a good man, and once while he was praying, the Lord spoke to him.

"Go to the street which is called Straight, and enquire at the house of Judas for one called Saul of Tarsus," said the Voice from Heaven, "for he is on his knees there praying, and he has seen in a vision a man named Ananias coming in, and putting his hand on him to restore his sight."

"But, Lord," said Ananias, "many have told me about this man, how much evil he has done Your people in Jerusalem. And now he has come here with authority from the chief priests to arrest all that believe on Your Name."

But the Lord said to him, "Go your way without fear: for he is a chosen instrument of Mine to carry My name to the Gentiles as well as to the people of Israel. For I will show him how much he will have to suffer for My sake."

So Ananias went to the street which to-day is still called Straight Street. Going to the house of the man whose name was Judas, he went into the room where Saul was praying.

"Brother Saul," he said to him, "the Lord Jesus, Who appeared to you on the road to Damascus, has sent me to you that you might receive your sight, and be filled with the Holy Spirit."

Immediately Saul felt as if scales had fallen from his eyes, and he could see once more. He got up and was baptized, and became a Christian.

The disciples in Damascus, although frightened of him at first, soon made him one of themselves. And Saul lost no time in telling his fellow-countrymen he was now sure that Jesus was the Son of God, and the Saviour of the world.

Everybody was amazed that the one who a few days before was trying to destroy the Christian faith should now be preaching it, and the Jews were so enraged that this clever and energetic man should now be on the side of the hated Christians instead of theirs that they laid a plot to kill him.

They put a guard on the gates of the city to catch him as he went out. But the Christians in Damascus lowered Saul in a large basket over the wall when it was dark, and he escaped to the Christians in Jerusalem.

The First Missionary

When he became a Christian, Saul took the name of Paul, and it is by this name we know him best.

The Christians in Jerusalem were at first unable to believe that Saul the persecutor had really become Paul the Christian preacher. One of the leaders of the Church, however, a good and generous man, called Barnabas, introduced him to the Apostles, and told them how Paul had seen Jesus on the road to Damascus, and how he had at once boldly preached in the Saviour's name.

How glad they were then to have Paul with them! All persecution ceased for the time being, and many Churches were formed throughout the whole of Palestine. Paul returned to his native city of Tarsus and was there for some time, quietly praying and preparing for the wonderful work that was before him.

After a while, Barnabas came to Tarsus seeking for Paul, and took him to the great city of Antioch in Syria. In this city there was a large number of Christians. It was in Antioch that the disciples were first given the name "Christian". It was given to them as a nickname by the people of Antioch.

Now, the Christians in Antioch remembered that Jesus had told His followers to take the Gospel to every creature, even to the uttermost parts of the earth. So they formed the first Missionary Society, and sent out as their first missionaries Paul and Barnabas.

Paul made three long missionary journeys altogether. He followed the great Roman military roads, and sailed the Mediterranean Sea, setting up Christian Churches in many of the large seaports, and working inland to form a chain of Churches throughout the Roman world.

He was sometimes alone, but often he had companions with him—Barnabas, Silas, Timothy, Luke, and others. It is Luke who tells us most of the many adventures and hardships of Paul the Missionary.

Paul tells us about some of them himself. Listen to what he wrote to the Church he had set up in the City of Corinth in Greece: "Thrice was I beaten with rods; once was I stoned; three times I have suffered shipwreck, a night and a day I have been adrift on the deep. I have been on many dangerous journeys, facing pirates on the sea, and robbers on the roads. I have been in danger from my own countrymen, and from the heathen as well. Many times I have been in much weariness and in great pain. I have often been kept awake by hunger and thirst, heat and cold. And, added to all these things, there has been the continual concern for all the churches."

Paul was the first missionary to bring the story of the Saviour to our own continent of Europe. Paul and Luke had come to Troas which was near the famous town of Troy in Asia Minor. Paul was uncertain where to go next, but one night, as he lay asleep, he had a vivid dream. He thought he saw a man of Macedonia (in Europe) coming to him with outstretched hands. "Come over and help *us*," the man was saying in tones of appeal.

In the morning, Paul decided this meant the Lord Jesus wanted him to cross over to Europe, and very soon they sailed for Greece, and arrived in the town of Philippi which was called after Philip, the father of Alexander the Great.

At the end of his third missionary journey, Paul returned to Jerusalem. There he was seized by the Jews and brought before the same High Council which years before had condemned Stephen to death.

But they could not condemn Paul to death, for he was a Roman citizen. Paul's father had received Roman citizenship as a reward for services he had rendered to the Roman Empire. So Paul, though a Jew, was a Roman citizen as well.

When he saw that the Jews were determined to kill him, he claimed the right as a Roman citizen to be tried by Caesar himself in Rome. So Paul made a fourth journey by land and sea, this time as a prisoner, to the great capital city of the Roman Empire.

On the way, the ship was wrecked on the coast of Malta,

Paul is shipwrecked off Malta.

and Luke's description of the wreck and their rescue is one of the great stories of the sea.

At last, they came to Rome where Paul was welcomed by the Christians there. He was allowed to live in a house which he rented. But he was chained all the time to a Roman soldier.

255

For two whole years, Paul lived like that in ___ ___. During this time, he preached to the Jews who came to hear what he had to say about the Saviour. And in that prison, too, he wrote some of the wonderful letters which we can still read to-day in the New Testament.

Luke does not tell us what happened after that, but it is certain that Paul was beheaded during one of the fierce persecutions in Rome under the wicked Emperor Nero.

One of the last letters Paul wrote before he died was to young Timothy. This is what he said to Timothy. *"For I am now ready to be sacrificed. The end of my journey is at hand. I have fought a good fight. I have finished my course. I have kept the faith. Now awaits me the crown of a good and faithful life which the Lord Jesus will give me on that Day. And not to me only but to all who love Him and long to see Him, as I do."*

Paul, although perhaps the greatest, was but the first of many, many missionaries who have taken the gospel to other countries, and to-day thousands upon thousands are continuing to carry the story of Jesus the Saviour to the uttermost parts of the earth.

THE END